DIANE DUNN

CUSCO
The Gateway to Inner Wisdom

A Journey to the Energetic Center of the World

Written in collaboration with Wendy Crumpler

 Planeta

Cusco: The Gateway to Inner Wisdom
A Journey to the Energetic Center of the World
© 2006, Diane Dunn.

Cover Design: Martín Arias
Book Design: Omar Portilla

All rights reserved
© 2006, Editorial Planeta Perú S. A.
Avenida Santa Cruz No. 244, San Isidro, Lima, Perú.

1st edition English, August 2006.
1000 copies.

ISBN: 9972-239-00-4
Depósito legal: 2006-6675
Editorial Project: 11501310600510

Printer: Quebecor World Perú S. A.
Avenida Los Frutales 344, Ate, Lima, Perú.

CUSCO
The Gateway to Inner Wisdom

For my parents
J. Norton and Fiora Dunn
Thank you for all
your love and support

Table of Contents

Prologue

I was ready. The panic in the pit of my stomach had transformed into a hollowness waiting to be filled. Seventeen of us sat in a circle on the ground in a makeshift soccer field carved out of the jungle. It was dark and stars sparkled above us through the clearing. The ayahuascero, the enigmatic jungle shaman who with his young daughter had boarded our long boat earlier in the day, poured his tea-colored brew into a glass and each of us drank about 5 oz. It tasted bitter, strong and earthy.

I sat on my mat and waited for the unknown, consciously relaxing my senses and releasing my physical tension. Soon the jungle noises rang in my ears like wind chimes, tinkling bells. In my mind's eye, flecks of color and shapes danced to this strange music I was hearing. My hands began to tingle and my head to spin. I took a deep breath and reminded myself to surrender and trust. Immediately an inner dialogue started that lasted for the duration of my amazing journey.

The voices I heard were my own levels of consciousness as well as wisdom guides, messengers, and loudest of all, God Herself. All were communicating with me, simultaneously. I was disoriented in my body and all my senses, yet capable of discerning and understanding all the messages at once. Nothing was normal. Many voices were talking me through what was happening, so I wouldn't be afraid. I didn't like being physically out of control, but the voices were so reassuring that I moved beyond fear like falling from a shooting star, and fell right into the loving arms of God. I heard her voice so clearly and felt her presence so close as to be connected, with nothing separating us. Then I felt nauseous. After checking with all my guides, I finally got up to move from the circle to the edge of the woods to throw up. The ground beneath me felt unsteady. When I opened my eyes, colors and shapes of nature around me looked more bizarre than what I was seeing inside my head. I crawled the rest of the way, threw up the ayahuasca, which was the only thing in my stomach, but continued to dry heave for what felt like an hour. During those choking coughs, I saw worlds and civilizations of horrors that needed purging. I understood things about human nature and evolution and transformation that I couldn't begin to explain in words. However, it gave this awful physical purging a dimension that felt healing and purposeful.

Eventually the voices told me that the purging was finished and I could stop it by using my breath. Each time I felt the desire to heave, the voices encouraged me to take deep breaths, reminding me gently that one of the most powerful tools for healing is breath work. They told me that I would use this in my healing work with others.

It was now time to rejoin the circle. As I moved back toward the group the conversations and insights continued to flow. I saw the place from which I originated; a multi-leveled world of angles and geometric shapes. It looked nothing like earth. There was nothing that earthlings would call "living" but there was a sense of great intelligence and wisdom. In that place, I too knew all. I could feel myself both as human and from that other place. I could look at human nature and laugh at our strange ways of complicating life. I knew that I had agreed to come to earth to assist with the healing and transformation of humanity. Therefore, I had become human. At that moment, I felt such peace being back in my place of origin and remembering who I really am and understanding clearly deep fundamental truths.

God remained with me. When we got to the subject of my intention I heard her say, "I know you want to see where you will be next and what you will be doing. I want to show you but it depends on you. It depends on what you choose." Just then, I heard a noise and opened my eyes. I saw a tall man standing behind the ayahuascero. It wasn't a man exactly but more like the ghost of a man, a bit transparent. I asked God, "Who is that?" and She answered, "It's part of your future. This man. But it depends on you. What do you want?"

"I want to do what I came here to do."

"You came here to be a healer and you can do that anywhere and in any profession. Know that whatever you choose, you will be a healer. You can't make a wrong choice so don't worry about that. You can stay in South Africa or move on from there. You can remain a minister, or you can move beyond church ministry. It's up to you. What do you want?"

"I want a partner whom I can share my life with, my purpose with. Where is this man? I want to meet him."

"There is a man who will be at the Conference in Urubamba. He is a very wise person, who has many things to teach you. And he will love you very much. He is like no one you have ever met before. But know that if you choose this, everything else in your life will change. Is that what you want?"

I knew this was not a casual question with an easy answer. I knew this was a contract that I would be committing myself to; something that I would be setting in motion. I took a deep breath. "Yes, that is what I want."

"OK. He will be there. And you don't need to look for him. He will find you."

The effects of the ayahuasca were becoming milder. My senses were feeling more familiar. I knew that normalcy would return soon. The voices were quieting down. But I was also losing that crystal clear connection with God. She was still with me but the veil between us was becoming more opaque. All the inner knowing I possessed in my place of origin was slipping away from me.

In its place was a profound love. Love so deep and wide, I simply floated in it. I felt so grateful. I felt grateful for love and life itself. I felt grateful for the insights I had been given, the visions I'd seen and for the indelible connections I'd made. I felt grateful for moving beyond fear and trusting in the amazing possibilities that lie on the other side of it.

"Know that if you choose this, everything else in your life will change."

And it did.

Introduction

My earliest childhood memory that I still picture so vividly is myself at three on a swing in our backyard. It was one of those incredible spring days in Cincinnati when the sky was a brilliant blue that cannot be painted and the sun was radiant, warm, and gentle. The air was alive with fragrance and the sound of birds singing. All around me was that green, that new green of everything as it first appears. The breeze caressed me as I swung higher and higher into the sky, as if I could fly with the birds. I was alive, I was free, and I was filled with delight that God could create such an incredible thing, this earth, this life, and the beauty of all of it. More powerful still, was the sense that I was a part of this creative miracle. The utter joy and wonder of such a moment is the connectedness you feel—the connection to God and nature and the understanding that you are a part of it all. Somehow important. I was completely present to God at that moment, and God present to me.

I was raised Catholic, so I'm sure at three I knew of God's existence and probably prayed each night some rote prayer supposed to give me clear knowledge of the might and power of God. But this God of the swing bore no relation to anything I had been taught at home or church. This God was love and acceptance and delighted in my being. This God got a kick out of my willfulness, my playfulness, my naughtiness, my imagination. This God was bigger than anything anyone had told me and I knew this God was in me and I was in God.

But growing up in the Fifties, my life experiences taught me more about limitations than expansiveness. Though I was being taught to think small and do as the others were doing, I had big dreams, secret dreams that I was sure my God of the swing supported.

I wanted to be an actress, not so much to be rich and famous, but so I could touch people's lives; make them laugh and cry.

I got married instead, deciding I could live the life for which I was programmed and be an actress on the side. Neither the marriage nor my acting career was very successful, but living in New York I discovered a whole new world where expansiveness was allowed amid the anonymity. When acting proved too frustrating, I started a theater company, thinking I could touch people's hearts with the plays I produced.

Still there was something missing, something pulling, something prodding. It always seemed to be just around the corner. If I could only get there I knew I would be happy. What was it, that elusive something? Was it a big theatrical hit? Was it fame and fortune? Was it a man to love me? Or something more?

I was yearning, a deep wide yearning that had no name. It felt like a sense of destiny calling me, a puzzle that had only a few missing pieces. If I could only find them and put them into place then I would be complete, then I could rest, then I could live happily ever after. At that time, the search for a soul mate came closest to embodying this mixture of longing, mystery and destiny, this thing that eluded me.

It kept me moving along a path of discovery that led me to an even greater understanding of love. Eventually I realized that I was searching for my highest self, not another person. I was seeking the oneness I felt with God and all creation that I first glimpsed on the swing. I was longing to discover my deepest calling, my life's destiny, a sense of purpose and meaning one can only find by expanding consciousness.

This book is about the mysterious proddings and unexpected adventures, that somehow were directing me, encouraging me, awakening me to new possibilities.

What I have now come to know, in the deepest part of my being, that I didn't quite understand then is that there is a wonderful powerful force in the universe (that I call God or Divine Creator, but known by many names), that conspires to assist us in our life's search for purpose and meaning.

The story of my discovery is a great adventure, filled with twists and turns, setbacks and surprises. This story however, is not just about me. It is about all of us learning to tune in to that unseen power—to see it, know it, and use it as an instrument of healing and transformation, to use it to discover our own inner wisdom.

Perhaps you've had some inkling of what I am talking about or you have a nagging suspicion that there should be more, some yearning that is not fulfilled by your current relationships with money, property, people, or things. By learning to access this mysterious power of nature itself, your journey can be no less fantastic or miraculous than the one I am about to tell you.

If you are aware that you are already on the path, I hope that this book may give you more steps to take to speed you on your way. If you are not aware of your own great adventure, this book is an invitation to go exploring, to be more alive and more yourself. In my memory of the swing, I knew that I was important, put here for some special reason. Of this fact I am more clear than ever.

I also believe that everyone reading this book has been put here for something special, particular to this moment in our cosmic history. We are perched on the edge of a great shift in the way we live, the dawning of a new era. As we discover our connectedness, not only to the mystical forces of nature, but to our oneness with all living and created things, we can recognize our special part in bringing about this amazing transformation.

At the end of each chapter, there are questions, answers, and exercises that have arisen out of the content of the chapter. If they are not your questions or you would prefer to just read the story uninterrupted, please feel free to skip the questions and return to them later.

SECTION ONE:

THE UNIVERSE CONSPIRES
TO ASSIST US

Chapter 1: The Impossible Is Possible

In 1987, nine years after coming to New York City to seek my fame and fortune as an actress and theatrical producer, I went to a psychic who told me, "I see you in Peru". At that time, I wasn't remotely interested in Peru and politely told her she must be mistaken.

Ten years later after graduating from theological seminary in New York and spending seven years as an outreach minister in Johannesburg, South Africa, I went to hear a visiting anthropologist speak about his many years working with healers and shamans in Peru. I was riveted. By intermission, I knew I had to go there. It had taken the Universe a long time to take me where I needed to go by a most interesting and circuitous route.

Looking back, I see many instances during those ten years where that mysterious force of nature worked its magic in my life, leading me to places I never consciously would have chosen. For example, a friend invited me to attend a Protestant church with her and, while I was skeptical that there would ever be anything meaningful for me at church again, I consented. That church had education seminars, one of which led me to start daily meditation and journaling.

After attending church for a while I began to grapple again with theological issues that had plagued me since childhood. Why was my experience of Christianity so judgmental while the teachings claimed that God is love? Who makes up the rules that say who's good and who's bad? How could I feel so connected to a strong spiritual force but so disconnected from the institutional church?

Again, the universe stepped in to lead me in the right direction. I reconnected with a man I'd met at church who was attending

21

Union Theological Seminary so I got to discuss and wrestle with those issues with a person not lofty and removed but warm, present, and as filled with the questions as I was. Our paths lead us in different directions but my need for answers was stronger than ever. I needed someone to talk to.

This was about the same time that I closed down my theater company, got fired from an advertising agency, and was unemployed for nine months searching for a meaningful vocation. I had plenty of time to talk to my friends and hear what was happening in their lives. Listening to the intricacies of their relationships, their searching, and their questions reawakened my fascination for how life works. I was truly interested in their situations and their questions. I felt somehow that I was more than just a trusted confidant. Advice I gave seemed to be helpful and I felt myself growing as well.

One night at dinner with a friend who had been with me through the ups and downs of job hunting, I excitedly told her about my latest "counseling" session. She looked at me and said, "Diane, you've been looking for a job in the wrong place. This is obviously what you love. Do this." I was stunned. How could I do that? I was 36 years old. How could I put my life on hold for three years while I attended school? I'd be 39 and starting all over again.

But the questions still burned inside me, so I made an appointment to speak with a minister named Leslie Merlin.

The morning of our appointment I had an unusually deep meditation. I felt God urging me to be especially aware that day for a message I needed to hear. When I got to Leslie's office, she asked me why I wanted to do spiritual direction. After listening to me tell her my life story of fighting with institutional religion, she said, "It sounds to me like you want to go to seminary. Did you ever think about that?"

The room shook. I was momentarily blinded by a light. My heart was pounding. I heard myself answer, "Yes, but I didn't think seminaries took people like me." She laughed and told me the story of how she ended up at seminary and all the people she met there that were on a journey of discovery just like mine. "There are," she said, "a lot of religious skeptics in seminaries."

I was shaking when I left. Surely that was the message that God wanted me to watch for, but it was too bizarre. How could I tell anybody about that conversation, let alone tell them I was going to go to seminary!

By grace, I had a lunch date that day with my friend Karen. As I rode my bike to meet her, I made a little pact with God (and myself). I would tell Karen about the meeting with Leslie and the idea of me going to seminary. My practical, sensible, straight shooting Virgo friend was also gentle enough to be trusted with such incredible information. She'd set me straight, but not make it too painful. If Karen thought it was a crazy idea, I'd just forget about it. If she thought it was possible, I'd continue to consider it. When I got to the restaurant I was still shaking. Karen sat in the booth across from me and when I told her the story, she burst into tears. She reached her hands across the table to grab mine and said, "Oh Diane, it's perfect!" She beamed her beautiful smile across the table at me, tears of happiness making her eyes shine like twin stars. It was as if I was in a dream. Had she really heard me? Didn't she know how insane it was?

I had been asking for some direction, and God's messages don't often get much clearer than that. However wacky it seemed, it would be ungracious to reject it outright just because it was totally improbable. It was impossible that I could take and pass the entrance exams in just a few weeks. It was impossible because there was no way I could afford the tuition. It was impossible because applications to Union were filed one year in advance. It was April and I wanted to start in September.

Improbable, yes. Impossible, no. I was accepted. Everything is possible! It still seemed preposterous but I had jumped in with both feet and a large loan. And it felt great. As soon as I got to Union, I knew it was exactly where I needed to be.

Are You Wondering?

Do you really think that anyone can make the impossible, possible or do you need special powers?

Anyone who chooses to be conscious and believes something is possible can make the impossible possible. Perhaps the question we should be asking is what makes something impossible? Often it is because there are powerful people or systems in place that make us believe a certain thing is impossible to do or to have. As this chapter illustrates, the impossibility of the situations were based on what I believed that I could do, rather than any outside force stopping me.

I have a friend in Lima. Her nephew wanted to go to Europe. He was 19 years old, going to school and working. He didn't have much money but he was determined to travel to Europe. Everyone told him it was impossible but he was not deterred. He decided as a first step he would walk to and from work everyday instead of paying 80 cents each way for the bus. It took him two hours each direction and every step of the way he thought about his trip to Europe. He saved 10 soles or about three dollars a week on bus fare. Of course he found ways to save money doing other things as well because his mind was set on his goal. It wasn't just a matter of money. He was determined to make the impossible possible. Three years later he was in Europe.

If you can imagine something for yourself then the impossible becomes more probable. If you take actions to bring about that probability, then it becomes more and more possible. That's something everyone can do, if they want to and believe they can.

Try This

Name something you want that you think is impossible or improbable. Everyday for 15 minutes, close your eyes and visualize it happening. Do that for one week. Then start taking actions to bring it about. See what happens.

Do you think life is predestined?

Each person comes into this life under certain circumstances, with opportunities and challenges. I believe this is where predestination ends and free will begins. In addition to one's material circumstances and corporal bodies, each person has a soul whose purpose is to awaken you to understand deeply the meaning of your life. As an individual, you have the opportunity to move beyond the given circumstances of your life to realize your potential, not just on a material practical level but on a spiritual level as well. As you expand your consciousness, you can recognize that you have both a personal and collective responsibility to heal, to progress, to evolve and to be of service in some form or another. When I took ayahuasca in the jungle, I asked the divine voice to tell me what I had come here to do. She answered that I came here to be a healer but I could do that in any profession and in any place. I think the specifics of your life's purpose are for you to choose.

My friend Bryan grew up in a working class family in Liverpool, England. He was the last of 11 children. He began working at the neighborhood butcher shop when he was 11 years old, part-time then full time. He learned the trade. There was no one he knew that had any great ambitions to be more than what was expected of them. Eat, work, drink at the local pub, sleep. But something in Bryan wanted more. By age 19 he bought the butcher shop. That was certainly a big mark of success in terms of his upbringing but still he wanted more. After a few years he decided to sell the shop and try his luck in London. He started out cleaning offices. Then he got a few clients of his own and hired some people to clean the offices. Soon he had a very successful business. But something still drove him. It was a search for deeper meaning in his life that led him to a Buddhist retreat center and eventually to Peru. He now lives a life of service and continues his search for deeper meaning and purpose.

Was Bryan's destiny to live the life of a successful butcher in Liverpool? He could have stopped searching but he didn't and he hasn't. His life did not follow the normal trajectory of someone with his background. In that sense he chose his destiny and continues to do so.

Try This
Ask yourself these questions. **Why am I here?**
What did I come here to do, to be, to discover?
Even if you don't always know the answer or the answer changes over time, the question itself causes you to look within yourself to uncover your own inner wisdom. Ask and keep asking.

Chapter 2: Amazing Grace

I didn't know when I began seminary, what I wanted to do when I got out. I wanted to be an ordained minister but I didn't want to work in a traditional parish setting. What I really wanted to do was to change the church into my vision of what Jesus intended. But not too many denominations were hiring (or ordaining) people for that sort of thing.

Life was so exciting at Union; I was content to just be there. My consciousness was being awakened on so many levels I could barely keep up. I was becoming a feminist, a preacher and a liberation theologian at what felt like breakneck speed. I was discovering the language to describe things I had known and believed all my life. I was like a dry sponge soaking up moisture. It was amazing. I was working hard to help create what was happening but I was also open to a wonderful powerful force that was leading me, guiding me, showing me the way. Often, the most important thing I had to do was say "yes" and stay open to all that was unfolding.

In my second year there was a course on liberation theology taught by James Cone, a dynamic black theologian, that brought new insight and more change to my life. Professor Cone began a lecture on liberation theologies in the third world, by saying that two-thirds of the world's population lives in Asia and Africa. He asked, "How does that reality impact the way you do theology or ministry?" I felt like he was pointing directly at me. His question hit with the same impact as Leslie Merlin's.

Maybe I could spend the summer in Africa, I thought, doing volunteer work somewhere to expose myself to another culture.

I had recently decided to go through the ordination process in the United Church of Christ. Their national office for Global

Ministries happened to be located across the street from Union. Perhaps they had some opportunities. I was new to the denomination, and this could give me a chance to develop a valuable relationship with one of the church's offices as well as live for two months in Africa. This was my thinking as I walked across the street and went up to the 16th floor.

Once again, the universe was conspiring to assist me. It was January 1990 when I first met Di Scott who worked in the Africa office of the UCC's Global Ministries. She greeted me with South African warmth and charm. It was nearly impossible at that time for U.S. church workers to get visas to enter South Africa, but she thought perhaps she could place me in one of the bordering countries where our church also had missions.

A few weeks after I spoke with her, South African President DeKlerk freed Nelson Mandela from 27 years as a political prisoner. That was in February. In March, Beyers Naude came to New York. He was an extraordinary Dutch Reform minister who defied his own church and heritage to fight against apartheid and human oppression at great cost to himself and his family. Di Scott had worked with Beyers in Johannesburg. She asked him if he could arrange a program for me and he agreed.

Beyers had been invited by Nelson Mandela to be on the first negotiating team to meet with the government to set up guidelines for the transition of power. Six months after DeKlerk's famous speech, there I was in South Africa, with Beyers Naude setting up my itinerary! I met people who had been through great hardship for many years, whose faith had sustained and inspired them despite the oppressive laws that stifled them. Sometimes it was too much for me to take in.

I kept asking God, why I had been given this incredible opportunity, to be in South Africa at such a historic moment, hearing the stories of so many people who had helped to bring about this enormous change. I thought of all the people in the States and Europe who had been involved in the anti-apartheid struggle for years, who would have given anything to be where I was. Why was I there and not someone else? It was a question I carried back with me to Union for my last year of study. I realized the answer was in South Africa and I wanted to go back to find it.

In August 1991 after graduating from Union, Global Ministries arranged for me to go back to South Africa as a Peace & Justice worker for one year. I worked full time for Peace Action, a local violence monitoring organization in Johannesburg. Because I was still preparing for ordination, I was "placed" (by divine assistance) at St. George's United Church in the inner city, to help with Sunday services.

Vernon, the minister at St. George's, was aware that I had done some community-building and small group work in New York and asked me if I wanted to do a "workshop" with the people who came to the soup kitchen on Friday night. I was still new to South Africa and not sure that any of my previous experience would be transferable. But I agreed to run a "sharing circle" on four consecutive Fridays after the soup kitchen.

That support group, as it came to be called, was a four-week commitment that continued every Friday for nine years. Because of my work with that group, the people of St. George's invited me to work full time developing a community outreach program for homeless and unemployed people in the inner city.

It was nothing I would have imagined for myself four years before when I was searching so hard for a new career path. It's not even what I imagined for myself when I was studying at Union. Yet it was the most challenging, rewarding, meaningful work I had ever done. As my best friend says, God gives you everything you ask for but nothing you expect.

Are You Wondering?

If the universe is conspiring to assist us, why doesn't God always answer my prayers or give me what I ask for?

Well, sometimes what you ask for is not always in your best interest. But even when it is, nature must take its own course. We are the only creatures on earth that have the power of choice. A lamb doesn't pray not to be eaten by the lion. It is the natural way of things. Humans must face the consequences of the choices they make and have made over time. Our choices are interconnected with each other, with those who have gone before us and with the environment in which we live. It is nature's way to balance itself. It is not a question of reward and punishment. Actions have consequences. They affect your life even if they aren't your actions.

Wanting God to deliver a specific result is not the same thing as the divine energy in the universe conspiring to assist you toward your higher purpose. So, if your prayer isn't answered, look beyond what you wanted for something else, for a different kind of answer. Raise your consciousness and expand your awareness. If you are aware and willing to make more enlightened choices, you will be able to affect the well being of others as well as yourself.

Try This

When you don't get what you pray for, pray again and ask to be shown a new direction, a new desire and pray for patience in the face of your frustration. The universe is attempting to assist you, even if you can't always see it. Change your perspective; imagine that God is answering your prayer even if it isn't exactly what you asked for.

Chapter 3: Born to Heal

In 1996, back in the States for a sabbatical, I attended a UCC churchwomen's conference in Boston. A delightful, buoyant, Lakota Sioux pastor named Marlene was also there. She glowed with enthusiasm as she led a session on Native American spirituality, which included an intriguing description of their ceremonial Sweat Lodge. Marlene explained that the womb-like dome was sealed with blankets with only one opening near the ground. After entering in a ritual manner on ones hands and knees, hot rocks are placed in the center of the dirt floor and the door is sealed. Invocations and prayers are chanted and water sprinkled on the rocks to create a cleansing steam. As she spoke, I longed to experience this communal sacred ceremony. Later she invited me to a gathering she was organizing on Rosebud reservation a few months later.

In that moment, I knew I was going. I hadn't the faintest idea where Rosebud was, who would be at the gathering, or how much it would cost to get there. What I did know was I would be able to participate in a Sweat Lodge. The lure of the Sweat Lodge turned out to be only the prelude to an adventure more significant than I could have imagined.

Although the gathering was an "immersion experience/sensitivity-training" for white Lutheran pastors working on or near Indian reservations, most of the week-long training was applicable to my cross-cultural ministry in South Africa and I was grateful to be included.

In retrospect, I'm sure the real reason I was at Rosebud was to meet Cecilia Fire Thunder.

Our first Sweat Lodge was just before we went to hear her speak. This dynamic woman embodied her name. Hearing-impaired from birth, her irregular speech patterns only enhanced her powerful story about growing up on that reservation. She was taken from her family, like other Indian children, to attend a church boarding school designed to strip her of her native language and spiritual heritage. She was later "resettled" with her family, to Los Angeles by a new Indian Affairs policy that believed moving Indians to an urban setting, would integrate them into the mainstream population. She laughed as she told us that all the Indians from different reservations soon found each other in LA and formed their own community simply to survive.

She laughed and cried with equally free expression as she told her heart-breaking yet inspiring story. Though she eventually became a very successful businesswoman, she kept hearing a call to return to the reservation, to help heal her people by helping them recover ancestral traditions. Their language and religious practices had been systematically taken from them, cutting them off from the connection to the divine creator so central in Lakota spirituality.

As her story unfolded, I felt a strange sensation in me. I was no longer in the midst of a large group. I felt the heat of a glowing white light that encompassed only Cecilia Fire Thunder and myself. Her background and life experiences were so different from mine yet I felt as connected to her story as if she was telling mine. I cried with sadness and joy at being recognized by her, as if she was the messenger telling me that I too was called to be a healer.

There were so many similarities between her people and the people I was working with in South Africa. Helping them reconnect with their own roots and ancient spirituality was such an important part of the healing process. Cecelia explained that the wounds were multi-generational (as they were in South Africa) and the painkiller of choice on the reservation was alcohol (which was also the case on the streets of Johannesburg). The only way to heal these wounds, she told us, was through an intimate connection with the Creator.

Similar to my meeting with Leslie Merlin, the minister who suggested I attend seminary, I was shaking when I left the talk. I knew I had received a message, a call to be a healer but I wasn't sure how I could do that, or what form it would take.

Rosebud Reservation is in South Dakota. The nearest airport is in Pierre. To get the cheapest flight, I stayed over some extra days. I'd heard about the Black Hills, sacred land to the Lakota said to have special powers and I felt drawn to go there. But they were more than 250 miles away. The universal force once again assisted me, when one of the group leaders gave me her rented car. I had never been to South Dakota before and knew nothing of the distances or the landscape between Rosebud and Rapid City. I set off with the name and number of a retreat center in Rapid where I could spend the night, no map, and only a vague set of directions. I planned to arrive with enough daylight to spend some meditation time in the Black Hills.

The whole drive there felt like a magical meditation. It was the strangest, most delightful feeling, like riding on gossamer wings through an enchanted forest, which in this case had no trees but other-worldly rock formations rising from the broken earth. I was alone but voices were speaking in my head, processing all the wonderful connections I'd made in the past week with an unusual clarity of understanding.

On the way, I stopped in a tourist shop and bought some meditation tapes one called "Spirit Winds", the other, "African Rhythms". When I got to Rapid City, I was stunned to find such a big city (since Pierre, the capital was so small). I had no idea where to go. I decided to stop and call the retreat center. I pulled into what turned out to be the Convention Center where they were preparing for a big Pow-Wow. The retreat center was fully booked. What now?

A woman using the phone next to mine turned to me and said, "Excuse me, I overheard you saying you were a minister looking for a room. I'm one of the organizers for the Ecumenical Social Action committee participating in the Pow Wow tonight and we have people who have offered their homes to visiting clergy. I'd be happy to arrange a room for you." Hesitant to accept such a generous offer, I said I'd try one other place the retreat center had given me but if they were also full I would accept.

I then overheard her conversation saying that the person who was suppose to bring the star quilts for the awards ceremony was unable to come and she didn't know where she would find replacements in time. While I was at Rosebud, I had uncharacteristically (and quite impractically) bought a beautiful, handmade, Lakota star quilt. Now I knew why. I offered her my quilt with the ease and grace of a person who knew it was all in the family. She gratefully accepted as I did her invitation for a night's lodging. We agreed to meet back in that spot in a few hours. She also promised to send me a replacement quilt similar to the one I was giving away.

As an afterthought, I asked her if she could direct me to the Black Hills. She asked me what denomination I was and when I told her she said that the UCC have a camp in the Black Hills and started to give me directions. She stopped in the middle and said it was a bit hard to find, directing me instead to another place just off the main road. I had only about two more hours of daylight.

The incredible connection with the woman in the convention center was simply an extension of what had been happening since I met Cecilia Fire Thunder. I headed toward the Black Hills, finding the UCC camp without even trying. I climbed a hill, looking until I sensed I had found the perfect spot for my meditation. I created a ritual, which arose from instinct rather than conscious experience. The silent meditation was incredibly beautiful and deep. It was a kind of ecstasy whose pleasure is derived from perfect stillness and peace in a place whose energy is pure power and spirit. Truly divine. I didn't want to leave.

The sun was setting however, and I knew I'd be stuck in the dark on the mountain if I didn't start climbing down now. Plus I needed to meet my new friend. I promised the hills I'd return in the morning before the long drive back to the airport in Pierre. I reached my car just as final darkness descended. The sky was midnight blue with a few radiant stars, not an artificial light in sight. Utterly peaceful. I felt charged with energy and an inner knowing that passed all understanding. I didn't have directions back to the city but I had something better. Perhaps you'd call her a spirit guide but her presence was so tangible she might as well have been sitting with me in the front passenger seat, reading me directions. And the way back into town was the least of it!

Driving back to Rapid City, I was listening to "Spirit Winds" on the car tape deck and a clear vision came to me of myself leading a healing workshop in the chapel of our church in Johannesburg. I saw us sitting in a circle with the same music playing on a cassette player. I was leading a guided meditation. I saw it happening. I asked my guide some questions about what I would do and how I would know. She told me to trust my inner knowing. She was clear that this was what I needed to do once I returned. So was I. The sense of power welled up in me like a balloon ready to burst. I felt like I could do anything I wanted with this power—the least of which was finding my way home in the dark, in a city I'd arrived in only hours before.

Then the balloon did burst. Perhaps it was because I had just passed out of the Black Hills into the city limits. Or maybe my self-conscious cockiness had slipped me out of the groove. In any case, I began to panic that I'd made a wrong turn and wondered which direction I was really headed. I did make it back of course but by now I was exhausted, like coming down from a drug induced high. I met my host for the night and eventually found myself sleeping in her guest room. I awoke in the pre-dawn dark, determined to find my way back to the UCC camp in time for sunrise.

Intention is everything. My morning sunrise meditation was just as beautiful as the sunset one had been. I felt such a sense of belonging, up in those hills—a sense of wonder and delight, excitement about the new future I was moving toward and the strange and wonderful coincidences that had led me to it. Once again I had to pry myself away, knowing that my plane had a time schedule. I took lots of pictures of that awesome sunrise through the pine trees and the sacred spot where I had sat under "my" tree. None of them came out. I wanted to capture my experience on film to convince myself it was real. Instead I held the memory in my heart, returned to South Africa and started our weekly healing workshop.

The format for these healing sessions took shape in the first few weeks. We started by sitting in a circle, with a lighted candle in the middle. We introduced ourselves by answering questions like, "what made me decide to come to the workshop today?" or "where do I feel blocked in my life at this moment?" Then I would lead a guided meditation, bringing divine light and love to the concerns people had shared. Afterwards, people were invited to comment on their experience or ask questions. Sometimes we would do an exercise using paint, clay, pictures, writing or some other creative experiment designed to tap into divine wisdom and healing light.

I had started my work in South Africa concerned with social justice and feeding the people, but I was moved by unseen forces to feed their broken spirits as well. I had heard my call to heal.

Are You Wondering?

How can I hear messages the way you are able to do?

You hear messages by listening for them, like turning your cell phone on with the expectation that at some point it will ring and a person on the other end will speak to you. If you have a sensation when you are invited somewhere (like I did when Marlene invited me to go to Rosebud), pay attention. Trust your intuitive response before the idea gets to your thinking mind. I have learned from past experience to listen to my intuition. Most of us are taught to turn it off, not to pay attention— especially if it is leading us to something strange, unknown or scary. So we choose not to listen, to turn off the reception. If you want to receive messages from your guides, your angels, your inner wisdom or from God, you need to spend time developing those relationships, just as you would if you wanted to receive regular calls from friends. Eventually the relationship will be strong and your reception will be so open that you begin to notice little things even in the midst of your daily activities. Something someone says to you in the grocery store, an article you read in the newspaper, an email you receive by accident or anything that seems unusual may be a gateway to new wisdom. Pay attention, observe what is going on around you and make quiet time to listen. Most of my messages come to me while I am meditating – with my inner cell phone on. (And the outside ones turned off!)

Try This

Make quiet time every day just to listen. Take time before you get up or just before you go to sleep. Make time to mediate each morning before you start the day. This is good practice to develop a deep relationship with your divine messengers.

Are there similarities between the Lakota American Indian and the Inka traditions?

Both traditions have a great respect for nature because they understand themselves to be part of nature, not dominate over it. Another similarity is they both give thanks before something occurs in anticipation of receiving their request. They both give thanks before planting in anticipation of a good harvest. They both acknowledge the elements: the sun, the rain, the animals, the fish. Both traditions are conscious about living in harmony with nature because they know their own well being depends on it. They both have special rituals and ceremonies to mark the seasons and special events in the community. They understand themselves in relation to the whole community, not primarily as individuals. They both have rich spiritual traditions that were nearly lost when they were conquered. Thankfully, those traditions have regained value within their respective communities so that we can also learn from their richness.

Try This

Practice giving thanks for what you want, as if it has already been given to you.

The Universe Conspires to Assist Us

As a first step to discovering your inner wisdom, it is important to believe there is a force beyond you that is helping you, not judging you. It is helping you to discover your best self, not punishing your every mistake. In fact, in this understanding there are no mistakes, only steps on your journey.

It is important because if you believe you are out there in this world all alone, or worse being tested with the expectation you will fail, then you are blocked before you begin. On the other hand, if you strongly believe that there is a force assisting you all the time then when you stumble or miss what you are reaching for, you can stop and ask how what just happened might be helpful instead of disasterous.

When I was out of work (for nine months!) and very frustrated because everything I tried didn't pan out, I was lucky to have a friend who shifted my focus in another direction. She helped me see what was happening in my life and not what wasn't. She also suggested I go back to school to study what I was already finding meaningful in my life.

Although the thought of going to a theological seminary, was not anything I would have imagined for myself at the time, it turned out to be the perfect choice for me. If I had not been listening to God's message during my meditation, with the expectation that whatever was going to happen would be in my best interest, it is unlikely that I would have spoken to Karen about the possibility of going to seminary. It is unlikely that I would have responded to my professor's challenge by going to South Africa. It is unlikely that I would have ended up at Rosebud Indian reservation to meet Cecelia Fire Thunder and start my own healing workshop as a result.

It is important for you to have the expectation and absolute belief that there is a creative power in the universe that is constantly assisting you. It is also important that you pay attention to it; that you develop a personal relationship with it; that you listen attentively and you don't judge what you hear from your limited perspective. This power sees and knows more than you do. Learn to trust it.

SECTION TWO:
TO DARE

1998 Solstice Celebration
in the Sacred Valley of the Inkas

Welcome friends and companions on this journey. We are in the "navel of the world," one of the most sacred places on planet earth. For this reason, we give thanks.

So, why are we here? Because now is the time of the great awakening!! This is why we are here—to become aware that we need to get into action, to accelerate the evolution of our becoming one with the universal spirit of the Age of Aquarius in the third millennium. Now is when our questions will lead us to the understanding of who we really are. We are gatekeepers of the winds of transformation, change and healing of the planet earth and all of her inhabitants.

There is nothing hidden in the Age of Aquarius. It is the revealing of mysteries. The great book of life is opening in front of us in numerous ways. We learn from the sky, the earth, the sun, the stars, the wind, the sea and nature. We are part of the divine Creator, and we possess all wisdom within us. Humanity is struggling to acclimate to what is new because they are afraid of losing what is old and familiar to them—all the things they have had from the previous Age of Pisces.

It is time to let go of everything in order to build on what is here and now, with love, light and truth. Then, the transformation will come. Let us conjugate the verb to be and not the verb to have and to stay. Let us take action. This is our great responsibility. But first let us work on our own purification and cleansing, just like the masters: Mayans, Inkas and all the great Asian cultures. In order to do this let us work with the four elements:

The Earth cleanses and transforms us. The Water washes and balances us. The Air purifies and enlightens us. The Fire transmutes and sanctifies us.

The cross of Aquarius has four equal arms similar to the Andean cross which represents the four elements and the four words of the Sacred Tradition: to Dare, to Want, to Know and to Be Silent. Let us work with the elements and the words to reach the center of the cross that represents our Center and total enlightenment.

(Excerpts from Opening Address delivered by Sergio on June 20, 1998)

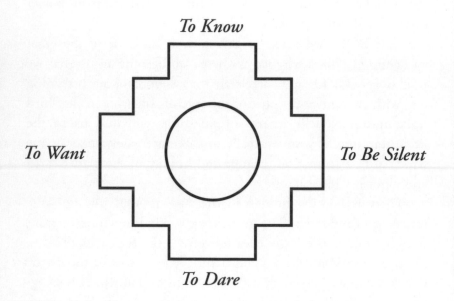

Chapter 4: The Four Words

From the beginning of time these four words have been used by many Sacred Traditions. When I first heard them, they meant little to me—only passing words in Sergio's moving and powerful speech. Since then I have recognized their power as fundamental resources on the journey toward deeper discovery.

The Chakana, also known as the Andean cross, is the ancient symbol of the Andean spiritual tradition. It has four equal arms that represent the four directions and the four elements. The Fire transmutes and sanctifies us. The Earth cleanses and transforms us. The Air purifies and enlightens us. The Water washes and balances us. Each of the four elements has a corresponding word: to Dare, to Want, to Know and to Be Silent.

We begin in the South, the place of FIRE. The Fire is also the sun, the source of life as well as the divine spark in each one of us. It is the most powerful of the four elements. It has the power to transmute. Transformation is a type of evolution, a kind of change that happens over time as we expand our consciousness and make healthier choices, alter our behaviour, retrain our emotional reactions. But Fire has the power to alter something instantaneously, in a flash. It changes not just the way we see and act and respond. It has the power to create something entirely new, to change the very structure of what we call reality. The Fire can transmute our heavy energy into golden light and love. It burns away the old so the new can emerge from the embers. The corresponding word is TO DARE. To realize our potential we must dare to change. To dare is to move beyond our comfort zone, to leap empty-handed into the void, to jump off the edge believing we will fly instead of fall.

Next is the West, the place of the EARTH, our mother, the giver of life. The Earth receives all our worries, doubts, frustration, anger, etc. as a gift which she uses like fertilizer to enrich her soil, where we plant the seeds of our intentions so they can grow and manifest. The Earth cleanses and transforms all our "shit" and uses it to nourish new life and growth. The corresponding word is TO WANT. To want something is to begin the process of creating it. Intention is everything. But what we want must be free to travel its own course, rather than held so tightly by our desire that we strangle it. To clearly name our want is a powerful creative act. Our intention must be clear and then released with love to fly its own course, which often if not always lands us in a much better place than we thought we were headed.

In the North resides the AIR. Air is our most essential element. We can go for days and weeks without food or water but without Air we will die within minutes. Air is also our most readily available element. It is given abundantly and freely everywhere we are and everywhere we go. It can expand our sense of time and space. It is the source of communication and connection. The corresponding word is TO KNOW. In Spanish the word is saber, which means to possess knowledge, to live our knowledge. It is related to sabiduria, which means wisdom. The path of transformation requires us to develop a knowing that moves beyond simply understanding a concept with our mind. To know, means to have such intimate familiarity with something that it becomes an innate part of our being.

We complete the four directions in the East, the place of WATER. The Water washes away the build up of heavy energy around us, our own as well as from others. Water helps us release and relax. It balances us. Water teaches us adaptability as it takes the shape of its container and goes with the flow. The corresponding word is TO BE SILENT. Without making time to be silent, we will never be able to hear the subtle urgings of divine support. In silence, with the breath, we calm ourselves, quiet the mind, and open to our inner knowing. We clear our energy channels and tune into higher frequencies.

The four sides of the chakana offer us ancient wisdom for this new era. We are living in the time the Inka prophecies called the taripay pacha, the time of meeting ourselves again. As we work with the elements and the words we will be able to reach the center of the cross that represents our divine center and the manifestation of this new age of peace, unity and prosperity.

When we do rituals in the Andean tradition we begin by calling on the four directions, starting with the South. Since the corresponding word To Dare is in the South, I will begin the next section with this sacred word. The most significant life changing events for me, were all born by such grand and little acts of daring: going to seminary, going to South Africa, going to Rosebud. However, my favorite act of daring which would seem modest by most standards, led to the most significant change of all.

Are You Wondering?

You said that Fire has the power to create something entirely new, to change the very structure of what we call reality. Can you explain that more?

Fire is the vitality of life. The sun is Fire at its most powerful. Fire lies molten in the center of the earth, yet it has the power to break through the crust and change the surface of all it touches. This same fire burns within you. It is your uncontained impulse, the source of your passion and desire. In a literal sense, when fire burns intensely it changes the structure of certain elements, like gold and silver and other metals. But I was speaking metaphorically in terms of how you can use the element of Fire to transmute the structure of your life, to use the spark of this fiery love to change the world and how you perceive it. This is a powerful element and as you learn to work with it, you can accomplish more than you ever imagined. Read on and the story will illustrate what I mean.

Try This

Get up at daybreak and go somewhere you can see the sun rise. Sit or stand in quiet reverence and wait for the sun to break the horizon. They say that it is only at this moment when we can look at the sun directly (eyes squinted), before it gets too high and too bright. Greet the sun and give thanks for its warmth and light. Recharge yourself with its energy. Feel its power—the power of elemental fire.

You explained the four equal arms of the chakana but you didn't explain the steps between the arms. What do they represent?

The three levels on the each side of the chakana represent the three worlds in the Andean cosmology: The upper world or Hanaq Pacha in Quechua, the material practical world or Kay Pacha and the underworld or UkuPacha. Each of these levels could also be said to represent the unconscious, conscious and super-conscious. They should not be thought of in terms of the Christian heaven and hell although they have some similarities. There is denser energy in the UkuPacha and lighter energy in HanaqPacha. But each has its place and its use. Each step represents an animal guardian for each level: The condor and the hummingbird in the upper world, the puma and the llama in the material world and the serpent in the underworld. There are also three principals that governed the life of the people: work/service (llankay); learned wisdom (yachay) and compassionate love (munay).

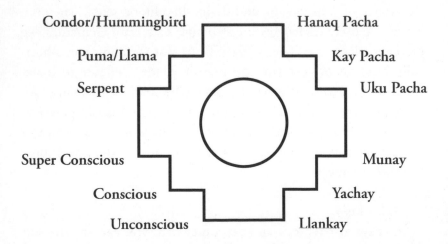

Chapter 5: Moving Beyond
Your Comfort Zone

During one healing workshop at St. George's in December 1997, I led an inner child meditation. As always, I participated. The instruction was to ask your inner child "What would you like to say to me today?" then write the response with your non-dominant hand. DiDi, my 3 year-old inner child, responded, "I'm bored. Let's have a little fun. I want more adventure. Whatever you do, even if it is work, have fun with it. Make time for yourself. It is all part of living life well. Creating what you want means living that way now."

A few weeks later, we were doing another workshop but this time the written dialogue was with God. The question was: what is blocking me from... [Fill in the blank]? I asked 'what is blocking me from finding my soulmate?' My left-handed God wrote: "You are limiting yourself by only going places you are comfortable. You must move beyond your comfort zone to open yourself to new possibilities."

Before concluding the workshop, I asked everyone to make at least one commitment to themselves and God, related to what we understood to be blocking us. I committed to do two things a month that were beyond my comfort zone and unrelated to work.

The night before, I had read an article in the local newspaper about a visiting anthropologist who worked with spiritual healers in Peru. He was giving a talk the following Sunday. I had actually planned to go camping that Sunday on my weekend off but I felt pulled to go to this event instead.

This may not seem like a big deal to most of you but there were a few things that made it quite out of my comfort zone. First, it was a fund-raiser, which meant that it cost about three times more than going camping for the whole weekend. Second, it was in a fancy northern suburb quite a distance from my inner-city home. I had such a dislike for the area (my reversed snobbery) that the few times I ventured up there, I always got lost, and the location of the talk was in an area I had never been. Both those things would have seemed less daunting to surmount if I had companionship but I couldn't get any of my friends to go with me. I hated going places by myself.

On the other hand, I had made this commitment to do something beyond my comfort zone and it did sound like it would be very interesting. So what if no one would go with me. I found the place without a problem and sat alone in the hall with 100 or so other people. I was riveted from the onset and knew for sure I had been directed there. My senses and perceptions were so over stimulated that I felt my face flush and my heart pound.

Alberto spoke about his many trips from the USA to Peru, first for his PhD research and later for his own voyage of discovery, learning from an Inka master the ancient ways of healing by working with image and energy, beyond the western frameworks of time and space. There were "channels of light" within the human body that were visible to certain shamans, he told us. The shamans were able to work with these channels, to see illness in people —physical, emotional, spiritual because they were all connected. They were also able to shift the energy within their patients in order to realign these rivers of light and restore health and well-being.

There were so many fantastic stories he was telling and even though I'd never heard anything like them before, there was a part of me that was screaming inside, "YES, YES, YES, it's true. I know this is true and I want to learn how to it too. I want to meet these people." There was such a sense of urgency within me I'm sure I could have gotten on a plane right then. During the break in the 3-hour presentation, I went to speak with him saying, "How can I go there and meet these shamans?"

He told me about a trip he was planning in June and promised to send me information if I gave him my address. The conversation was brief and he moved on to the next person in the line of people waiting to speak to him. I wandered away as if in a daze. I stood on the line for tea repeating to a woman I'd never seen before, "I'm going there. I'm going to that place. I mean I'm really going there." I'm sure she thought I was nuts. Part of me thought I was nuts. But I was also never before more sure of anything.

I was going to Peru. I didn't know how, I didn't know when, but I knew I was going. I woke up the next morning with my mind racing and full of all the possibilities and problems. I didn't have any dates for the trip that he had described to me. I knew it was sometime in June, but I was scheduled to be in New York for the celebration of my parent's 50th wedding anniversary. The timing might not work at all. Still, I had been given so many amazing opportunities in my lifetime and this felt like one of them. On some level, I knew it would change my life in a dramatic way.

Weeks passed and I heard nothing from the group organizing the trip. When finally a package from the United States arrived I tore into it like a starving person and devoured the information. The trip appeared to be everything I had hoped for and even more—a weeklong event with shamans and healers from North and South America gathering to celebrate the Winter Solstice.

Then, disaster. The dates overlapped when I needed to be at my parent's anniversary party. I was crushed. I read through the entire packet trying to find another trip that interested me, but nothing connected. It was that one or nothing. Disappointment engulfed me. Maybe there was the slightest chance, if I could get my family to change the date of the anniversary party by two days. I'd still have to leave Peru before the conference ended, but maybe, maybe that could work.

However, I couldn't imagine my mother going for it. She is a lovely and gracious woman, physically beautiful even in her late 70's. Still, she came from an era where things were done a particular way, where etiquette and form reign supreme, and familial obligations are attended to without question. How could I possibly miss her 50th wedding anniversary? I emailed her and the rest of the family to check out all possibilities, but let go of any expectation regarding the outcome. If it was meant to happen, it would happen and if not….

I expected at best Mom might agree to move the date of the party a few days and include with that a gentle but firm reminder of the importance of family. What I got was this.

"Dear Diane.

Isn't it always the way, good things always seem to bunch up on each other. The opportunity to go to Peru and be with a group of people who mean much to you both personally and professionally certainly sounds like something you shouldn't miss. So go with our blessings."

It was less important to my mother that I be at the New York party than the fact that I could make it to the week at the Outer Banks of North Carolina that she had planned for family only which started June 27th, the day after the conference ended. In actuality the timing would be perfect. I could truly have everything I wanted. I had received an answer from my mother. Not the answer I expected, not what I had asked for. No, something much better.

And that was that. I was going. There was even a pre-conference trip to the Amazon jungle that I could take which also sounded interesting.

I wondered if the pull I felt to go to Peru was related to finding my soulmate, but I didn't have much time to ponder because a crisis arose at work. Glen, the manager of Homeless Talk, a newspaper written and sold by the homeless community, had embezzled the project's funds. His scheme unraveled when the bank mistakenly called me to say that the account was overdrawn. It was then we discovered he had systmatically emptied our entire savings, including a rather large grant. With Homeless Talk money Glenn purchased an expensive 4x4 truck, of which he had sole use. The day before I got the call from the bank, Glenn resigned but still had possession of the truck, all the Homeless Talk computer equipment, and the cell phone.

In addition to Homeless Talk, I was also dealing with some problematic people at our church's housing project. I woke up stressed out. When I sat down for my meditation, I remembered my suggestion to a woman I was counseling, to imagine the next few days exactly as she wished them to be. I decided to practice what I preached and began a wonderful meditation.

I saw Glenn peacefully handing over the keys and the phone. I saw people at the church coming to deal with their housing issues and me peacefully connecting with them, without anxiety. Then I began to imagine how I could spend the weekend. A spirituality workshop that was on my schedule had been postponed. I had hoped my long awaited prince might be there but alas, I was dealing with Glenn instead!

I saw myself on Sunday and Monday at a beautiful country inn I went to occasionally, Quiet Mountain Guest House. When I came out of the meditation I was floating in the light, sure everything would be fine, one way or another.

Instead of "fine" I got a day full of miracles. I spoke with the bank, the auditors, and the people who had given us the grant and still had time to call Quiet Mountain to book a room for Sunday. I bought bread for our soup kitchen and headed for the church, still calm and centered and right on time.

Once there, I learned that Glenn refused to come in with Homeless Talk's possessions. I offered to call him and I was able to speak with him in such a calm, caring, reasonable way that he agreed to meet me, if I would come to a designated spot about 25 minutes drive from the church. I agreed without knowing how I could manage, without another driver. Just then, one of the refugees living in our housing project came down to see me. He had a driver's license. Soon we were on our way.

Glenn was waiting just where he said and very peacefully gave me everything. The whole day had gone exactly like I imagined it. On a day of serious crisis and disruption, I had been completely calm and everything worked as if I knew it would. The funny thing was, I hadn't done the exercise expecting it to work! Just doing the meditation had shifted my anxiety. That was relief enough. But having it really work that way... well maybe I was already learning the ways of the shaman.

The idea that I could manifest reality simply by envisioning it fascinated me. Just for fun, I tried it again. During my meditation,

I saw myself at Quiet Mountain with a man. When I came out of the meditation I realized what a ridiculous notion this was. Quiet Mountain was a place that mostly couples went to for a romantic weekend getaway. In the six or seven years I'd been going there, I never saw a single man there, let alone on a Sunday night. I simply let it go. Instead, I asked for a little sunshine to brighten the overcast day.

I left Johannesburg feeling relaxed driving through the beautiful landscape. Just as I turned onto the dirt road leading to Quiet Mountain the sun broke through the clouds. A nice looking blond man helped me remove my bicycle from the rack when I arrived. Amazingly, Frits, a divorced businessman, was there on his own. He explained that his daughter and son-in-law had booked the room at the inn for the weekend but they had to cancel, so Fritz went instead.

He intended to leave Sunday morning but Saturday had taken his new BMW for a drive down a nearby dirt road. Driving too fast, a stone flew up and punctured the fuel tank, which he didn't realize until he was preparing to leave. The repair people were fixing the car when I arrived. By then Fritz had already decided to stay another night.

He invited me to join him for dinner and we had a lovely evening together. He wasn't really the man of my dreams but I couldn't help thinking some little elves out in the cosmos were having a good laugh. Think we can't manifest even the impossible? We'll show you! I had a good laugh myself. I also realized a very important part of manifesting one's visualization had to do with being unattached to the outcome or at least the size and shape of the package it is delivered in.

I had the principal down pat by now but the art of its delicate balance was something I would learn over and over again in the next two years.

A few days later I got my itinerary for Peru. Arrive in Cusco, June 14th. Machu Picchu overnight on the 15th. Return to Cusco on the 16th and link up with the group going to the Amazon on the 17th, then return to the conference in Urubamba on the 20th. It was set.

And the Amazon trip was being led by Daniel, a shaman from California. Maybe that was the connection I had been searching for.

Are You Wondering?

How did you know it was important for you to go to Peru?
Over the years that I have been meditating, I have learned to trust the things that come to me. This was especially true with the meditation we did during our healing workshop. So, when I heard the message that I needed to move beyond my comfort zone and open myself to new possibilities, I took that seriously. When I read the article in the newspaper, I was very interested to hear about alternative healing by shamans in Peru. The location and cost was sufficiently out of my comfort zone, which encouraged me to go. Once I was there, listening intently to what was being said, my whole body was vibrating. I have rarely had such an intensely visceral experience to information. I knew in every part of my being that I would go to Peru to meet the people about whom the anthropologist was speaking. And since I am open to such things, conscious of them, I took this intuitive sensing very seriously. Did I know what was going to happen if I went to Peru? No. But I did know that it would be important, whatever happened. And of course it was.

Try This
Next time you have an urge or intuitive sense to do something that seems beyond your comfort zone, dare to do it.

Can anyone manifest their day the way they want it?
Well, anyone can attempt to manifest their day the way they want it. I can tell you that I haven't manifested a day since, quite so spectacularly as I did those two days! That experience was a unique sort of test for me, I think. It made me a true believer. If you can visualize something, then it is possible to manifest it. Even if what you visualize doesn't happen just as you saw it, you

have still set something in motion that may lead you in the right direction. I'll give you an example of something that has happened in the last few days. I am organizing a big event and there were three people I really wanted to come. In fact, I was inspired to invite them during a mediation. I visualized clearly at least one of them coming. I was very disappointed when they declined my offer. But in the process of sending the invitations, I was communicating with someone who worked for them. That connection may turn out to be just as important for our event than if the others had accepted my invitation. It is important for you to visualize your desires and intentions because it is daring, because it says you believe that such a thing is possible. It is good practice and good experience. The more you do it, the better you will get at it.

Try This

Make quiet time in the morning before you start your day. Visualize your day exactly how you would like it to be. At the end of the day, review what happened and see how it compares to what you visualized.

Chapter 6: Immersed in Peruvian Magic

The actual trip to Peru was long but uneventful. I had good seats the whole way and even got to sleep a bit, a blessing as the best priced flight I could get took me to London and New York before Lima and finally, Cusco. My Lima flight arrived in the city about 4 A.M.., the same time as various other flights, so several other people gathered with me at the gate awaiting the connecting flight to Cusco. I noticed a group of three men and a woman traveling together. The men were looking for a place to smoke. I deduced they were from California and felt judgmental about that and their smoking. But I also found one of the men attractive and oddly familiar so I watched them intently. We arrived at Cusco and they were behind me in line for passport control. For a moment I wondered if they were also in Cusco for the conference but they were obviously not spiritual enough to be doing that so I listened a while longer, then forgot about them.

My Peruvian travel agent, Tito, had sent a young man named Teddy to meet me at the airport. He drove me to my hotel but offered to come back later and show me around the city. At the hotel, I was given coca tea to help with acclimation to the altitude. Teddy changed money for me, told me how to get to the square, and suggested a cafe where I might get breakfast. My one year of high school Spanish was enough to order ham and eggs and coffee. Later, when I walked around the square shopping at the numerous stalls full of sweaters and jewelry, weavings, and wall hangings, I found that some of the street vendors spoke a bit of English. I saw a lovely silver and turquoise cross with four equal sides and a circle in the middle. I felt compelled to buy it. I had purchased my first chakana without knowing its significance.

The city was marvelous. From the first glimpse of Cusco as we descended through a gap in thick clouds hanging on Andean peaks to the 400 year old Spanish architecture built on 800 year old Inka ruins, I was mesmerized and fascinated with everything.

I returned to the hotel to nap. Though the elevation of Cusco is 11,000 feet, Johannesburg is about 6,000 so acclimation wasn't problematic for me. On the other hand, it had been a very long trip and I was tired. Teddy arrived later in the day to guide me through the city. He had recently graduated from the University and was therefore, a qualified tour guide. He took me up narrow streets, telling me both Inka history and his own. He was troubled by the conditions of poverty in his country and guilty about his own status as an educated young man from the middle class. His job taking wealthy tourists hiking three to four days on the Inka trail had exacerbated his sense of disconnection from his homeland.

It was such a special connection between us. I told him about the conference I was about to attend and asked if he knew the shamanic tradition of the Andes. He didn't. But I could tell I had touched his longing to know more about his restlessness and his roots. He had gifted me with his knowledge of Inka history and I had given him a gift in return. I didn't know it at the time but we had just practiced ayni, the act of reciprocity central to the Andean tradition.

That night my dreams were intense. In the first, I was pregnant and my belly was growing rapidly. I couldn't figure out how it had happened because I hadn't had sex with anyone. But people were gossiping and I wondered what I could do. It occurred to me that I could have an abortion if I didn't want the baby. That's when I woke and the dream changed to flying, soaring in all directions. Free, free, free. In another dream, I returned to my house, though not my real house, with my friend "Tudor" to find it had been broken into. Windows had been broken and things moved although they were stacked somewhere in the back. I was particularly upset because they had broken a stained glass window.

I was up early the next morning to catch the 6 A.M.. train to Machu Picchu. It was a beautiful ride first up the mountain to

13,000 feet, then into the Sacred Valley of the Urubamba at 9,250 feet. The train stopped in the little town of Aguas Calientes (Hot Waters) where the 250 passengers of the train disembarked to take busses up another 1000 feet to the ruins. There had been a guide on the train with us who now took the 15 of us who were English-speaking on a tour of the ruins for about 3 hours. I could have listened for hours more to this archeologist who had worked on the site for over two years.

How do you describe energy? And how do you describe wonder? I was filled with both as I wandered through the massive mystery. I walked and climbed and touched and smelled. Every cell and every pore drank in information both literal and energetic. The majority of the crowds left to make the three o'clock train, but I stayed on. I climbed to the highest point of the ruins themselves, the women's cemetery, and turned around to view the site from above. How splendid and how cosmically perfect. I chose a spot for my meditation the next morning. At 4:30 I boarded a bus for town, exhausted from all the physical exertion, but energized on a deeper level. My body hummed.

I took a nap at my hotel then walked up to the hot springs that I knew existed here. Well, I knew they existed, but I didn't know where or what the protocol was. My travel agent had told me to bring my bathing suit and I was directed to a tall hill as the most specific direction to the baths. The narrow cobblestone street I climbed ran by the river and was full of little shops and restaurants. I noted one that I thought might be a good choice for dinner on the way back down. The shops grew fewer and the area more remote as I climbed until finally the river and the mountains were the only things in sight. I wasn't sure it had been the best idea to head out on my own to this nebulous destination. Then, suddenly as the sun was setting, I was there. I bought a ticket from a person who spoke no English, changed into my suit and surveyed the pools. There were several, all with sand bottoms. I got into the biggest, not knowing the difference between them. As I entered I spied a handsome young man with a ponytail and asked in English if he knew the difference between the pools.

He didn't but he had responded in English, albeit with a Latin American accent. I eventually tried the other pools and worked out which was the hottest. I spoke to a Chilean Indian man I had seen up at the ruins who was moving from pool to pool. He said I should move from the hot pool to the cold pool three times for ritual cleansing and I followed his advice. Each time moving to the cold pool got easier.

Mostly, I was at ease with myself. Though I wasn't a person who generally enjoyed doing things by myself, here I was feeling liberatedly alone. Free to talk or not talk as I desired, delighted not to be around other North Americans, and having my own personal adventure. I felt like a child climbing into a tree house... the world was mine. My aching body relaxed. I was peaceful.

On the way back to my hotel I stopped at the restaurant I had seen earlier and ordered a chicken dinner. The young man with the ponytail entered and we ended up sitting together. His father, who spoke very little English, joined us and though he seldom talked to me there was a sense that he understood everything that was going on in the conversation. They were Chilean, and Gonzalo was a student about to complete his studies in architecture. He spoke of his concern for the growing materialism in his country and his respect for life, nature, and South American history was genuine and heartfelt. Both of them were interested in the work I had been doing in South Africa and the conference I was about to attend in the Sacred Valley. Once again, the connection was easy, flowing, with a sense of give and take that I had earlier with Teddy. How easy to connect with people in this mystical place.

The next morning I took the 7:30 bus back up to the ruins. I wanted to do my mediation before the crowds arrived. I faced the valley with Huayna Picchu to my left, meditated, and wrote in my journal, all while sitting at the edge of a 1,000-foot drop to the river flowing far below. When I finished, I crossed the ruins to climb the magnificent peak to the East, called the Gateway of the Sun, the temple at the top of the Inka trail. It is an arduous climb and I had already had a bit too much sun. I ran out of water on the way to the top but some inner determination and the stunning view kept me climbing. It was a different sort of meditation I was engaged in now, a connection to the mountain itself. I reached the summit grateful for the cool shade and the chance to rest my aching calves.

When I descended, I again met Gonzalo and his father, Armando. You would have thought we'd been friends for years the way we greeted each other. In that conversation, Gonzalo reminded me that everything happens for a reason. Of course, I knew that already but I was sure I'd be remembering his words as well as our lovely connection that evening when I returned to Cusco. After all, I had the night off to rest, relax, and recuperate from my strenuous hike.

I ate lunch at a little sidewalk restaurant in the village before boarding the three o'clock train back to Cusco. I noticed the group from California that I had seen in the airport and was grateful they boarded the car behind mine. They were loud, and I wanted peace. Actually, what I wanted more than anything at that moment was a shower and a nap. I had traveled to Aquas Caliente and Machu Picchu with only an overnight bag and was desperately in need of a change of clothes.

Shower, nap, and getting my stored clothes were my plan as I entered the hotel lobby which was abuzz with activity. This was the headquarters for the pre-conference excursions as well as hosting another group that had just returned from a two-week trip. As I made my way through the hubbub, Jose, one of the conference organizers grabbed my arm and said, "There you are. We're having a meeting in ten minutes with the group going to the jungle."

This was an unexpected change of plans. I had been told I would join the group tomorrow in Lima. I expected to meet them at the airport for our flight to Porto Maldonado.

Meeting or no meeting, I had to have a shower. I bolted up to my room and jumped in the shower. But I was faster than my suitcases, which still had not arrived when I got out of the bath. By the time I dressed and found the meeting room, I was ten minutes late.

I hurried breathlessly into the room then stopped, stunned. I was going to be traveling down the Amazon with the group from California. No, it couldn't be. To add to my shock Jose was explaining how and when we would be taking the ayahuasca.

What? No one said anything to me about ayahuasca! It was a purgative, hallucinogenic jungle herb brewed by special shamans. I had read one man's rather harrowing account of his experience with this jungle root and thought, "I could NEVER do that!" One of the reasons I didn't do drugs in college was because I do not like feeling out of control. Yet here I was in a room with this group of Californians about to go into the jungle for the sole purpose of doing ayahuasca. Things always happen for a reason indeed! Only the warm, familiar presence of Teddy, my guide from days before, kept me calm as adrenaline shot through my body. Now what?

I stayed to listen to the group leader but my head was still spinning. Daniel, the leader, also from California had been working with nine of the fourteen of us headed to the jungle for as long as ten years. They had been planning their Amazon trip for the past two years and he didn't seem at all happy about including outsiders in his group. If that's how he felt, I thought, why had he accepted me when I wrote my entry application from Johannesburg?

I was feeling more and more uncomfortable. When Daniel asked if everyone was okay and looked directly at me, I shot back, "No, actually I'm not. I'm a little flipped out because I didn't know we would be doing ayahuasca." The room was silent but the reaction couldn't have been stronger if all of them had yelled, "What!" at the same time. They looked at me as if I had six heads. The leader, who was also stunned, suggested I speak to him privately after the session.

As the group broke up, Nancy, the Californian I had seen in the airport with the two men days before, came over and hugged me. She asked if I wanted to join them for dinner when I was finished. I was touched by her warmth and kindness. Others followed suit and offered hugs and words of encouragement. One on one, even Daniel seemed warm and compassionate.

He suggested that I think about whether I wanted to do the ceremony with them. It was my choice. I said I would sleep on it, but a part of me knew that I had been drawn in a powerful way to this trip when Jose had mentioned it months before. I felt confident that I would choose to do it.

Our wake-up call was for 4:30 but I awoke at 3:50 with terrible diarrhea. Was it yesterday's sidewalk lunch or fear of the jungle? Certainly yesterday had been an exhausting day, physically and emotionally. I wasn't sure I was prepared for another turbulent day, but I didn't want to deny myself something that might be a significant experience either. I left the hotel with the others at 5:30 for the airport. I sat next to Arthur from Germany, the only other "outsider" who had been part of the group the night before. He had decided to join the trip at the last moment and this would also be his first ayahuasca experience.

My physical discomfort continued and grew during our lengthy wait for the plane from Lima, but it was miniscule compared to the travel that came next. Our plane landed at Puerto Maldonado, a small jungle town on the Madre de Dios river in the southeast corner of Peru. We were met by a rickety bus with open walls and wooden benches for seats. A short and, for me, thoroughly miserable ride into town brought us to the side street where we were to rendezvous with Don Ignacio, the 72 year old ayahuascero master who lives in the river valley. Others wandered through the town while we waited. I lay on the hard wooden benches of our bus and tried to sleep, then found a makeshift toilet to use before our boat ride down the river. Don Ignacio arrived accompanied by two young daughters. He spoke no English and in fact spoke little at all even in his own language. Our translator was Marco, a lovely Peruvian man who had come with us from Cusco and seemed, like Don Ignacio, very relaxed and gentle, very low key.

The ride to the river was only a few minutes but the boat ride to our final destination was long, long, long. Perhaps the fact that we were traveling at the breakneck speed of about two miles an hour was irritating me. But two hours without a place to rest my back would have been difficult for me under the best of circumstances. My vision of this trip had been lush green vegetation, brightly colored flowers, pristine waterfalls, and jewel-like birds flying overhead. What I got was a horribly overcrowded flat-bottom boat with plank seating traveling down a brown muddy river on a gray, clammy day. Normally I would have been running the "I paid a thousand dollars for this?" dialogue in my head, but all I could really think about was how physically bad I felt and the fact that I was actually going to take ayahuasca that night.

After an eternity in the boat we finally reached the small landing of our jungle eco-lodge. Thank God, at least I would get some respite from the gloomy river in my little two-person cabin. I lugged my bags up the wooden steps to the lodge area where there were about twenty small cabins. I had brought too much stuff and a lot of it the wrong stuff. I had expected the jungle, you know, hot and humid, not cool and clammy. And I still felt physically awful. "Oh, please, just let me get to my room and relax," I thought.

I pictured myself being able to drop down on the bed and rest a bit before lunch, but when I got to the very basic and rustic cottage I realized that the mosquito netting over the beds would preclude much getting up and down. There was a hammock on our tiny screened in porch, but the thought of swinging to and fro was less than appealing at the moment. There were also two angled wooden chairs on the porch but the surface of everything was dark and damp. Inside the cabin were two beds, a sink, shower, and toilet, and one narrow shelf. The only other place to put anything away was the floor. Inside was dark and outside was dark. I longed for sunlight and felt claustrophobic.

Lynn, a woman from Florida, was assigned as my roommate. She was a tall, thin, blond sales rep for a cosmetics firm. Unbelievably she had brought a whole supply of beauty products with her. "Oh, brother," I wondered, "Is this ever going to get any better?" She just didn't strike me as the kind of person who would be interested in exploring her spirituality, and I expected to dislike her or tolerate her at best. But all my judgments were being challenged on this trip and this was no different. She was very interested in my work in South Africa and we got along amazingly well.

After settling in our rooms we met in the dining room for lunch. The tables and chairs were sawed-off log stumps, heavy and uncomfortable. Though the food was good, my stomach was still too upset to eat. We were told that this would be our last meal until after the ayahuasca at eight that night.

We met as a group to talk about the ceremony. Daniel explained that the ayahuasca could cause you to purge with diarrhea, vomiting, or both but that part passes. It was important to move beyond that, release fear, relax, and not "fight" the ayahuasca. Then you could more readily learn what the experience had to teach you. Also, it was important that each of us be clear about our personal intentions for doing the ayahuasca. We would name what we wanted in advance of the ceremony as a way of claiming it and calling it into being. This would help us later.

Once we started going around the circle sharing our intentions, I felt more at home. It was like being at my own weekly support group in Johannesburg. It gave me greater insight into the people of this group and again I felt judgments melt away. I began to trust that our leader was committed to us all and wanted each of us to have a good experience. The intentions were lovely, many having to do with discovering a life purpose. I was clear. I wanted to move beyond fear and connect with God, the source of all power. I wanted to feel that power —to know it, in order to use it for healing. My second intention was also clear. I wanted to see and know what work I would be doing next and where. The energy in the circle was very strong, positive, and uplifting when we finished.

I returned to my cabin and climbed through the mosquito netting for a much-needed nap. When I woke two hours later I was feeling better. I was peacefully resigned to the fact that I was, indeed, going to take this mind-altering jungle "medicine" in a few hours, but I would not say that I was excited by the prospect. When my roommate returned from a nearby island inhabited by rescued domesticated monkeys and wanted to tell me all about it,

I could feel my anxiety level begin to rise again. I asked for some "quiet time" and she respected that. I prepared for the ceremony by writing in my journal and praying for guidance. I gave thanks for the willingness to move beyond my fears and to enter the unknown trusting in God's grace. I wished that Don Ignacio had been available to us beforehand for questions, but I had heard that he was a wise and powerful shaman and I had to trust that.

Most of all I focused on my stated intent: my desire to know what work I would be doing next and where.

We gathered at eight o'clock and walked to a clearing a short distance from the dining hall. We placed our ground cloths in a large circle and sat as Marco translated the private conversation Daniel was having with Don Ignacio. We were asked to note who was on either side of us as a way of looking after each other. Other than a few instructions we were in silence—all our questions had been addressed at the session earlier in the day. Now it was time.

We were instructed to stand as Don Ignacio handed each of us in turn a glass full of murky liquid. I was the next to the last person and waited nervously for my turn to come. When finally it was my time, I drank with surprising calmness. Arthur was the last person. When he drank, we all sat to await our experiences. I closed my eyes. How long a few minutes can seem especially in cool semi-darkness, especially when you are waiting for the unknown. I waited.

"Okay, nothing's happening," I thought. "Well, that's fine, I tried, I was willing. Ha! All that build up for nothing."

Then music, a tingling, tinkling. A shape, now two, colors moving, intersecting, intertwining, dancing to the chimes and crystal ringing. Voices coming out of the darkness in my head, voices from different levels of existence. "Oh, my God. This is it. Here we go." "I can't go, my head is spinning." "This is fine, everything is fine." "Oh, how beautiful, the color." "Let go now, the experience has begun." "All that you want to know is available." "Relax. Breathe." My body melted and expanded into the earth, the air, the dimensions of being from which the voices came. I slid through space and time into the consciousness of God. And she was me and I was her and her voice was the most clear and present of them all.

"I'm nauseous," I told us all. "Do I need to move to the bushes now to throw up?" "Yes, this is good." "Are we ready?" "We are with you." "We are ready." "Are you sure?" "Yes. Breathe. All is well." "You can go now." "Yes, okay, let's go." "It's time. Go now."

Then moving, a hand, a foot, connecting to an earthly body of which I was a part, moving in it liquid, energy flowing to nerves and bones and muscles, liquid energy.

Eyes open. "What is this?" "All is well." "Oh, this is too bizarre, nothing looks right." "Breathe." "Move your feet. All is well." "The earth is rubber." "All is well." "You're doing fine. Just keep moving." "Oh, my God, the grass, the trees, they're geometric." "I have to close my eyes." "Breathe, we are with you." "Where are my hands? Are these my hands?" "I'm going to throw up." "Yes, that's right, go ahead now. It's fine." "It's too fast. It's coming too fast." "Yes, it's fine, you're fine." "The others?" "Yes, do you hear them?" "I hear it all, I see it all." "Yes, you're here with them." "I'm in the jungle. I'm throwing up now."

And I can see that it's just the liquid I drank nothing more. And I can see that it's worlds and nations and hurts. And there's more. My body pushes up through me, through my mouth come horrors and indignations, putrid, gangrenous, sad, tortured. I don't want it. "Yes. You're doing great. That's what it is." "I'm choking." "Breathe, We are with you." "Release it all. It must be released." Civilizations, dimensions, lifetimes, disruptions, cataclysms, through me, through my stomach, out my throat. Out. Out. "That's it. That must be it." "No, there's more." "We're not finished yet." "Can I stop now?" "Things can be healed, they must be released." "This is transformation. We must do the work." "You're doing so well, keep breathing." "There's more." "I'm gagging, I hear myself choking." "Breathe. All is well."

Chanting. "Oh, the ayahuascero. He is helping. He sees." "You can come back now." "You don't have to be alone." "I don't have to do it all?" "It is finished. Breathe." "Breathe through the nausea. It will pass." "Remember to breathe, it is the key to healing." "You will use this in your work." "Yes, you did well." "Thank you." "We are finished."

Moving, peacefully, on rubbery ground. I inhabit a body. I inhabit a body now, not always. No more body. Light, free, ahh! Home! My place of origin, I see it. The place beyond death. High, far, many levels, angles, light, peaks and steps. I float, I rise, I remember. Levels of energy and dimension. "What is this place? no bodies?, no life?" "Shh. I remember. No human life, but my life. I remember." Peace. Calm. Wisdom. Knowledge. Clarity. All. I am home. I am restored. I am at peace. I look down from high above and smile at my earthly incarnation. Humans — small, fragile, limited. "Why do humans make their lives so complicated?" A knowing presence is with me. I recognize him, my counselor. He reminds me, "You chose to be human." "Yes, I know but what a pleasure to be back here where it is so much easier to see and understand again. Why do humans get so stuck? Don't they see?" "You have a purpose. Remember. Healing. Understanding. Compassion. Help them to see." "Love, yes. Love is the key. I remember."

I float back down. Down, down back to the jungle. Human. Body. Love within me. God present. Peace. Silence.

"OK. I'm ready. I want to see it. To know where I go next in this life."

"Are you sure you are ready?"

"Yes, I want to know. Show me." A sound, I turn. A shape behind Don Ignacio, an energy body, a man. "A man? Is it a man?"

"You wanted to see. This is part of your next step."

"A man?"

"Yes, there is a man but it all depends on what you want. He is very wise and will love you and never leave you. He has many things to show you and teach you. I know you want to see where you will be working and what you will be doing. I wish I could show it to you but it all depends on you, what you choose and who you choose to be with. The place and the particular thing doesn't really matter. Whatever you choose and wherever you are you will be doing what you came here to do, which is to be a healer. You can stay in South Africa or go somewhere else. You can be a minister or move on from being a minister. The partner you choose will determine these things but know that there are no wrong choices. Whatever you choose is okay. Trust that."

"But this man?"

"Know that if you choose to meet him it will change your life completely. Is that what you want?"

"Yes, that's what I want."

"Very well, then. He will be at the conference. You need not look for him, he will find you. But you must remove your resistance and be open. Do you think you can do that?"

"Yes."

"Then it will be."

The voices had quieted and God was moving back behind the veil of consciousness, but I had heard all and known all and been connected to the source. It would never leave me completely. I had been changed.

Around me I heard and saw the others of my group, some purging, some chanting or crying out. I was aware of them and aware of my own body, cold and tired. When Daniel came to each of us to see how we were doing, I said, "It was wonderful."

We moved back to our cabins about 1 A.M.. and though I felt nauseous I kept reminding myself to "Breathe, breathe." It was one of the lessons that stayed with me most clearly from the experience, the healing power of breath.

In the morning, I told the group that I would not be doing the ayahuasca again with them that evening which was the plan. Everything I needed to know, I had already learned.

I told no one about the figure I had seen behind Don Ignacio or the promise God had made me. I held it in my heart like a secret wish. Could it really happen? Could all the waiting and the wanting and the dreaming I had done be at an end? Who was waiting for me in Urubamba?

Are You Wondering?

Do you really think God is a woman?

God is neither man nor woman nor any earthly creature and yet God appears to us in many forms – male, female, flower, bird, breeze, and spirit. God has been made manifest through Jesus, Mary, Moses, Buddha, Krishna, Mohammad, and saints of all varieties. Probably it was a female God who spoke to me in the jungle that night because I had experience in visualizing a female God. The theological seminary I attended has an inclusive language policy that insists that students and faculty speak of God in gender-neutral terms—which is to say no one could call God "he" or "she". This was a new concept to me. Like most of us, I was raised to think of God as "father"— an old man wearing a white robe who lived up in heaven. In order to break my habit of thinking of God in only masculine terms (and inadvertently breaking the seminary rule), I decided to try imagining God as female. The image that came to me was a woman who reminded me a little of my grandmother (who used to put me on her lap and tell me how much she loved me). I was only going to use this image to neutralize my familiar male-God image but I was so comforted by this warm, understanding, loving, female God that I often continued to visualize her in my meditations. I did however, learn how to speak, write and understand about a God who is beyond gender. It was very liberating. This "language policy" led me to expand the limits I had placed on God and to connect with God in a more meaningful and amplified way.

Try This

Close your eyes and visualize God in at least three different forms, different from the ones with which you are most familiar. Note how you feel with each of these images. With which one do you feel most comfortable, loved and supported?

Do I have to do something I am afraid of doing to really change my life?

Yes, because change is scary. If you avoid doing things because you are afraid of them, then you can't grow. The irony is that we live in a world that is changing all the time but humans tend to resist change as long as they can. Better that you become an active player in life by choosing change before it "happens" to you. We have a natural instinctual fear of the unknown. This is what you must dare to move beyond. By doing so, you become the author of your own fate, the creator of your own choices, the producer of your own possibilities. With each fear you choose to pass through, you become more confident. You learn to trust your intuition and by doing so you develop your inner wisdom which becomes your divine guide. Do what you are afraid of doing consciously, and it will change your life for the better.

Try This

Think of one small thing you would like to change and identify the fear that is preventing you from making that change. Then, move beyond your fear and do it anyway.

Chapter 7: Meeting the Masters

Two days later our group rose at 4:30 to travel up the river, to get the bus, to get the plane, to get another plane, to get to Cusco. This time the travel was a delight. I had made friends with many in the group and we had so much to talk about. When we arrived in Cusco we had time to explore a bit and eat lunch before collecting our belongings and boarding the bus for the one hour drive to the conference in the Sacred Valley.

Not everyone was going. Several of the group were headed back to the United States and our partings were teary and heartfelt. How could it be that I felt so deeply after only four days? Hard to believe this was the same group of Californians that I had wanted desperately to avoid less than a week before in the airport.

The Sacred Valley was such a relief after the darkness of the jungle. The physical beauty of the place took my breath away just as it had on my trip to Machu Picchu. I loved being surrounded by those mountain peaks, like benevolent old souls looking down on our gathering.

The conference center was also light years away from the tiny dark cabins in the Amazon. Here, we were in the lap of luxury by Peruvian standards. There were several motel-like units, each with several rooms, each room with a bath. Ahh, hot water, now there's luxury. As we entered the lobby area of the main building that Saturday afternoon, there were two sandwich boards, one listing room assignments, and the other listing conference events for the day. I found my name on the room list and was happy to see that another of the women from the jungle that I liked a lot would be my roommate. While I was there looking I perused the board to try and discern which men were single by seeing who was rooming with whom. Just paying attention, not really looking.

That evening, June 20th, the opening address was given by a tall bearded man from Lima named Sergio. The power, authority and love with which he spoke, moved me deeply. I felt myself responding with the same "Yes, yes, that's how it is!" that I had felt months before hearing the anthropologist's speech in South Africa. It was a vision, a call to transformation in the new millennium—the very thing I had been praying to be a part of. With such an auspicious beginning, I knew this conference was the life-changing event that I had imagined it might be.

The speech provided a framework for the whole workshop and created sacred space in which we could work. Most of the people who attended had some previous experience with shamanism. Sergio's words reminded us that we were all here in this life at this moment for a very important purpose, to recover the simple but magical ancient way of life in the Andean tradition.

Sunday morning was the Winter Solstice, the most sacred and important day of the Inka calendar. I arose at 5 A.M.. to go with a group to a special sunrise ceremony at the ruins of Ollantaytambo. There was music and dancing and four stations where we did despachos (the traditional offering to the elements) with the Q'ero elders. The Q'ero Indians are from very high villages of the Andes. Because of their remoteness, these villages were not catholicized by the Spanish in the 16th century with the rest of Peru when the Inkan empire was brought to an end. They have maintained many of their ancient shamanic traditions and are said to be the purest practitioners of that art. In the hierarchy of Andean priests they are highly respected. To be blessed by them during the ceremony was a great privilege.

I got to be at the station with a revered and high level Q'ero shaman, Don Manuel. After he and his assistant, Don Francisco, had laid out the despacho the rest of us were invited to place three coca leaves in the arrangement that signified our intentions or desires. After that the despacho was folded and wrapped in a woven cloth and the elders used it, along with their medicine bundles called mesas, to cleanse each of us of heavy energy. It felt so wonderful as they passed the bundles over my head and down my front and back. Then the sun burst through the clouds to warm the chilly morning and we all danced. I stood beside two attractive men and wondered if either of them could be the person I was to meet, but I remembered the message that he would find me and I made no effort to engage either of them.

When I got back to the conference center I attended session after session with healers, shamans, and energy workers. Some were incredible, others merely okay, but not once did some dark, handsome stranger approach and take me in his arms. After two days of not meeting the man I had been promised I was getting depressed. But then I went back to the small town of Ollantaytambo and in the ruins there found a stone in the perfect shape of a heart. It was so beautiful and felt like a gift from God reaffirming her promise to me. I released a little of my "need" to know.

That day, Tuesday, two other things happened that were important to me. I mentioned to one of the conference organizers that I would love to study Inka spirituality in Johannesburg. She told me of a woman living in Johannesburg who was interested in forming a group there. If we could plan something with enough people, we might get the very same anthropologist I had originally heard to do a workshop with us. The prospect made my whole body start to hum. I knew I could organize it and get enough people. My years of producing theater in New York City had been a perfect training ground for such a task. All I needed was some possible dates to do it and I'd be off.

The second thing, later that night was a session led by Don Ignacio about ayahuasca. During that session he did a part of the chant he had done with us in the jungle and for a moment I was back there enmeshed in visions. He also said that when taking ayahuasca with a group, he can see each person's experience. He could tell if someone was having difficulty and needed him to chant or rattle or do something to ease the way. I had felt him do it for me when I was purging. He explained through his translator that this ability to see another's experience was more than the physical. He actually knew their entire experience with the ayahuasca, every part of it.

He knew my experience! Then he had heard God speak to me. He could tell me if it was real. Obviously, other people wanted to ask the same question. I stood in line to speak to the ayahuascero. Arthur was in front of me and I knew he had had a bad experience. He asked Don Ignacio what the problem had been. Don Ignacio replied, "You weren't open and you got stuck. Men often have more difficulty crossing over than women." It was a simple answer and I'm not sure it was what he wanted to hear.

Then I got to ask about my incredible adventure. "What would you say about my experience?"

"It was normal."

Normal! Normal! God spoke to me like Moses on the mountain, surely he had something more to say. "Then I can trust everything I heard?" I asked him.

"Oh, absolutely. Trust"

That was the reassurance I needed. If I could trust then my partner was still here and everything was fine. I could wait.

On Wednesday, many of us went into Cusco for the Inti Rami celebration at Sacsaywaman, the Inka fortress above the city. We got there at 11:30 and the pageant didn't start until 2:30. We sat for hours in the wooden bleachers. Finally, I walked around the crowds, which I really enjoyed, but I was definitely ready to leave at 5:30 when the ceremony was finished. Some decided to stay for shopping and dinner, but I took the bus back with the majority of the group to return to the conference. I was starting to feel edgy. Tomorrow was the last day of the conference and still no man.

I had wanted to take a session on Andean meditation that evening, but it had been cancelled as so many of us were late returning from Cusco. There was a ceremony down by the river that I went to, but after a few moments it didn't feel right to me, so I left. I ended up meeting Marco and my jungle roommate Lyn, and going to the bar to have a drink. While I was sitting there a strong arm came out of nowhere and wrapped itself around me from behind. When I turned there was one of the attractive men I had noted during the Winter Solstice despacho in Ollantaytambo. He pulled me to him and hugged me close. It felt so good, so powerful. "Him!" a part of me thought, though it didn't seem possible in another part of my consciousness that this was the man of whom God spoke.

The energy between us was very strong. We walked to the river, sat on a bench in the darkness, held each other, kissed, and talked. We talked about coming to Peru, about the conference and what it had meant to us. He talked about his girlfriend.

Girlfriend? My first response was betrayal. How could he do such a thing to me? Then I realized that he had done nothing to me other than engage me in some light romantic pleasure. I had been looking for romance and the universe had merely obliged with a pleasant experience not so deep as to defer me from my original intent. This was not my partner, but I did not need to reject the loveliness of what it was by feeling angry about what it wasn't. I laughed at my old patterns and released on yet another level. Tomorrow was the last day of the conference, but tomorrow I would look for nothing.

In the morning, I had planned to do a session on the Black Madonna but the session on Andean meditation had been rescheduled for the same time in the hall where the opening address had taken place. I wanted both so I went early to check out the spaces. First, I walked into the meditation room. The lights were low and colored candles burned across the front of the stage. The energy was gentle, flowing, peaceful. I crossed the concrete courtyard to the room with the Madonna session and the energy was completely different. I couldn't tune in to it at all. I walked back across the way to the meditation hall, went inside, breathed, and knew I would stay. On my way in I noticed John, a man I had spoken to the night before during dinner. He too was having difficulty deciding what to do. We both stayed.

We were briefly introduced to Regis by Jose who was translating because Regis didn't speak English. Regis had a gentle unassuming manner and with little fanfare, requested that we leave space between each chair and sit comfortably, feet on the floor, eyes closed, relaxed. In the beginning of the meditation we were eagles flying over the Andes from Pisac to Ollantaytambo, to Machu Pichu. As the meditation continued, he moved among us. I was aware of his strong, loving presence as it moved passed me and I felt transported from my small life among fears and worries to a freedom and openness calling me to my higher self. He spoke to us of all humanity becoming as one and how love and light were the only things that mattered. Even in the bliss of that meditative state I was aware of how similar to the opening address in tone and power this message was. Though he spoke in Spanish and we heard his words through an interpreter, there was no separation from the love that he bestowed on us. Slowly he brought us back down from our journey through the skies of our own consciousness and we rested at peace.

He stood beaming his love to us from the front of the room, that beatific half-smile that showed his gratitude and delight with the energy that had flowed through him and been transferred to us. Then he asked if there were any questions.

Questions, I wondered. Questions about what? It was lovely, everyone felt it, what could there possibly be to question? We sat in a little more silence than was comfortable when finally John spoke up.

"I just wanted to say thank you. I was really not in a good place when I came in here and I feel so much better now. Thank you."

Regis looked at John with the eyes of a hawk. Looked deep into his heart-center and pointed directly at it.

"You, have a brother, an older brother. And you are very angry with that brother. You need to release your anger because it is blocking your heart-center and it will make you sick."

John's face went pale, then red as if struck by a bolt of lightening. It was clear from his face Regis had read his innermost feelings and thoughts.

The room was frozen, stunned. No one had told us to expect anything like this. Suddenly the questions flew.

Everyone wanted to know what Regis saw. One man was told he had a big heart but needed to heal a sadness related to his parents. A woman who had visions of a cat biting her neck was assured that it was merely a part of her femininity she had been denying that needed to be reintegrated.

I was shaking. Could he see me? Could he see what was in my heart? I wanted to ask, no shout, could he see it? I wanted to know so badly that I could barely find the words or get them out of my mouth. "Can you see if I am doing something to block my desire?"

He looked at me with such love and benevolence all others in the room disappeared and I was no longer afraid to ask him anything. "Which desire?" he asked me. "You have many desires."

"My desire for connection." I told him simply.

Again that look, into my heart, into my soul. "We will talk afterwards, " he told me. Afterwards? Privately? Why? What did he have to tell me?

We stood in the room next door a bit later looking for the interpreter to help us, but Jose had disappeared. A woman from the group volunteered to assist us but when she had difficulties with some of the words, Regis stopped her. No. We must wait. The information he had for me was too important. It had to be translated exactly.

I felt uncomfortably special as he kept me close by his side while many others approached him for answers to their questions. He was calm and patient. When finally Jose returned to translate for us, Regis told me, "You are a beautiful person. You have so much love and are very giving. But you can also be gullible. It is good because you are trusting and open, but you have gotten hurt."

He paused and looked at me. When he spoke again it came from a place deep inside him. "Human beings…" he sighed, "…they do things. Mean, hurtful things sometimes. But that's not what matters. Only love matters, unconditional love. I know men have hurt you in the past but don't hold on to that. That is not what is important. Only love is important. Continue to love unconditionally without expecting anything in return. This is the only thing that really matters."

I asked him again about connecting with a partner.

"Love and trust," he told me. "Trust your first perception. Your intuition is strong and right. Trust it."

The connection with him was true and strong and loving. The healing I felt went far beyond his words. I recognized his specialness among so many gifted healers. Moments later I ran into John and he shared his story about his brother. I shared my story about my search for a partner. I knew now that it was fear that had been blocking my desire, fear of being left, being hurt, making the wrong choice. I was crying and felt so open that everything just spilled out of me. I felt free, released from a heavy burden I'd carried for many years. I felt loved, healed, and affirmed.

I was shimmering with the release of energy as I walked to the river for the next ceremony. I saw Regis on the way and, without the aid of an interpreter, he told me to take a stone and wash it in the river. Then when I felt my energy out of alignment I could put the stone on my forehead to rebalance. I went to the river to look for my stone and found four more heart stones. It seemed I was being reminded that love is everywhere.

After that ceremony I noticed the anthropologist's girlfriend walking away from the river. I still needed to find possible dates for him to come to South Africa for a workshop and she suggested we go up to the conference center right then to speak with him. I left the river with her without washing my stone. On the way, though, Regis saw me and pulled me over to him. Sergio was with him and translated for us.

"Did you forget what I told you about the stone?"

"No, I'm going now back to the river," I told him as I showed him the heart stone I had chosen. He took it from me and put it in my other hand. Then he handed me a beautiful smooth white stone. I knew it carried his energy and would be a great aid to me in my own energy work. I washed both stones in the sacred Urubamba.

The final two ceremonies of the conference were a despacho with the Q'ero elders and the closing healing ritual, back to back.

First, the despacho. The Q'ero were in the middle of the floor. I sat in the front row to be able to see everything. At the end we put in coca leaves with our intentions and mine was to trust everything God had told me in the jungle about my new life unfolding. After the despacho there were three stations for cleansing. The first station was the Q'ero elders, the second, women healers, and the third station were the men including Regis and Sergio. The workshop participants traveled to each station to be blessed and have our energies adjusted. Each station held a different experience for me. It was great to be blessed by the Q'ero once again and when I went to the women's station, one of the healers did an energy adjustment on my sternum and spine, which generated an intense heat all over my body.

At the men's station Regis and Sergio again adjusted my energy and dotted my forehead with some type of flower oil. I felt such a strong energy from both of them. Out of all the healers at the conference, they were the two people to whom I had responded most strongly. They transferred such power and peace and joy and freedom. And such love. I was filled with awe.

Finally the closing ceremony of what had been a remarkable conference. There were candles, speeches, poetry, and music. Then hugs, tears, laughter, promises. Love is the only thing that matters and there was love all around.

Then, the icing on the cake, I spoke to the anthropologist and cleared dates for him to come to South Africa in January. My work at the conference was done and my new life was beginning. OK, I wasn't going home with my partner who was suppose to have found me at the conference. But maybe he had found me I just didn't know it yet.

Are You Wondering?

What are the "simple but magical ways of the Andean tradition" that Sergio spoke of in his opening address?
Working with the elements of nature and the mountain-energy may seem simple and basic to city dwellers, but to the

people who inhabited these mountains for a thousand years or more it was what sustained them. Because the people had such a deep connection with their surroundings, they understood the importance of living in harmony with nature and respecting divine creation. They knew that living in correct relation with the natural order, they would be provided for. They gave thanks before starting any project with the assurance that Pachamama would give them a bountiful return on their investment. The tradition teaches that each element: earth, water, air and fire has properties beyond the functional and material. As you learn to work with the elements, you discover not only their hidden powers but your own as well. Each mountain has its own special energy and spiritual significance. The tradition teaches that the "apus" (spirits of the mountains) can assist you, protect you and guide you. When you connect deeply with the elemental forces, you discover the "magic" they possess.

Try This

If you live near a mountain or a river, go to it and spend 10 minutes a week (or more if you like) connecting with its energy. If not, go sit outside on the ground and connect with the spirit of the earth (Pachamama). Tell the mountain, the river or the earth what is happening in your life and what things you would like to change. Give thanks for their assistance and support, assured that the support will be there.

Why didn't you consider that Regis was the man you were told you would meet at the conference?

I didn't think it could be Regis because I assumed that the man I was told about would be a romantic partner. Regis didn't fit into that category for me, so it didn't occur to me until much later that he was, in fact the one. It is a perfect example of how you can miss some very important opportunities in your life because you are looking for something else. You can fail to see the value in what is being presented because you are focused on what ought to be, rather than what is. Lucky for me, I did recognize the deep and powerful connection I had with Regis and stayed in contact with him. The opportunity was still within reach.

Try This
The next time something doesn't go quite the way you wanted it or expected it to, look for the treasure inside your disappointment.

Chapter 8: Going on Faith

I returned to Johannesburg with my heart full of the wonderful adventures and insights from my trip. The healing workshops at the church were now opportunities for me to share what I learned in Peru. I wrote to Regis thanking him for the time we spent together and how much he had helped me. I mentioned the Inka Spirituality workshop I was planning in Johannesburg for January 7th through 10th, led by the anthropologist who organized the Solstice Conference. Perhaps Regis might consider coming to South Africa, the letter suggested, for a workshop that I would be happy to organize, for I wanted to learn more from him. I wrote a similar letter to Sergio, especially thanking him for the inspiring opening address that he had given.

Basking in the glow of my Peru experiences, however, was soon overshadowed by realities closer to home. Several problems were arising at work. My good friend and colleague Vernon, who was pastor of the church, was thinking of resigning from the ministry. In addition, several problems had arisen with our housing project. Except for the healing workshop and other 'healing' aspects of the ministry, I became less and less excited by my work and increasingly stressed out by it.

In fact, one day it got so bad I sat down for an inner dialogue with DiDi, my inner child, to see what was really triggering the stress. She said, "I can't do what I want! I just want to practice what I learned in Peru. I want things to change but I'm panicked because I'm not sure what that means. So I keep doing the old things but they feel uncomfortable."

Meanwhile I was having strange, vivid, intense dreams that I wrote down and discussed with my spiritual director, Michelle. DiDi may not have felt I had time to practice what I learned in

Peru, but my dreams were working overtime to shift and process all that the trip had set in motion.

I also began concretizing the January workshop by booking a retreat center, gathering mailing lists and emailing the anthropologist to confirm his arrival and program. I was getting indications he wasn't sure that he could come, and if we didn't start advertising soon, it would be too late to organize. Though not knowing if he would come was frustrating, when he finally told me in late September that he couldn't make it, I wasn't surprised. Oddly enough, I wasn't even disappointed, and stranger still, I decided to hold on to the venue a little longer, just in case something changed.

Problems at the church continued to plague all of us and I became clearer and clearer with each passing week that I wasn't going to renew my contract with Global Ministries, my employers in the States. I had a dream in which I was staying at a friend's house. She told me I couldn't stay there anymore. I reacted very calmly even though I hadn't yet found another place to go. Oh well, you can always rent something, I thought. My gradual unspoken sense that I would probably be leaving South Africa at the end of 1999 became a full blown decision during one session with Michelle.

I had a cold that day and I knew, for me, colds were really about sadness. Michelle asked me what I was sad about. I told her about the latest trauma at the church but soon heard myself say I was sad because I would be leaving. Not just that was I leaving a job that had been so meaningful for me, but a stable job with a good salary, health benefits, and a pension! It meant I would be leaving my beautiful little house, my car and all kinds of material stability I'd never really had before as an adult.

We also discussed my identity as a minister and how that might change. I told her how I was drawn to the kind of mystic, energy healing that Regis did in Peru. By the end of our session it was clear to me that I had already decided to leave. In my deepest self I was confident that the new thing would be better, more full and more complete than what I was currently doing. At the same time, I was scared because I couldn't see what that work was or imagine where it might be.

Two days after the 'cancellation' of the January Inka workshop, I received an email from Regis in Spanish. It had been a month since I had written him. A friend translated it for me.

"Dear Diane,

"I received your letter and feel great satisfaction that the universal force is with you and that you are the recipient of cosmic harmony. This means that now you have amplified your consciousness and you now understand that your existence on this planet earth has as its mission, to expand the light of wisdom and to go establishing the truth, the spiritual force among human beings.

"As a citizen of the world, I travel to distant geographical points of the planet and I go there, where my presence is needed. Therefore, I accept with much gratitude your invitation to go to Johannesburg from January 7-10. You organize the form and timetable of the work and my participation in the event, I am sure will augment the energy and light in Johannesburg.

I suggest you also invite Sergio who gave the opening address and participated in the closing healing ritual. This I give you for your consideration.

"I have been thinking very much about you and your great spiritual sensibility. In this respect, I tell you that only when the disciple is prepared, does the master come.

Your friend, Regis"

I was stunned. To get both Regis and Sergio together for a workshop, now that would be something. I was so excited about the workshop that I didn't fully digest the other parts of Regis' message. I wasn't thinking about my "amplified consciousness" or "my mission to expand the light of wisdom" which seemed a bit grand from my current perspective. But to plan and attend a workshop, that I could do.

My only problem now was I didn't have a clue what they had in mind. I wasn't even sure if Sergio could make it. I spoke to a woman who had organized workshops with visiting mind/body/spirit celebrities. She gave me helpful advice and encouragement to go ahead, and told me that Jo-burg's one esoteric magazine where I could advertise the workshop was preparing their last issue of the year. The deadline for ads was the previous day but she suggested I call them anyway and gave me the number. When I phoned they told me if I faxed the information to them in the next hour they could still put it in.

I hastily made up a three-sentence classified ad about Peruvian shamans coming to teach Inka spirituality, listing the dates and my phone number. The next day I designed a flyer, using the English translation of Sergio's Opening Address for inspiration and a picture I'd taken of Machu Picchu. The truth is, I invented the content of the workshop without having the faintest idea what they intended to do or even if Sergio was actually coming. I just kept visualizing the three of us together at Common Ground retreat center with 50 or so other people.

The next day, I faxed Regis a letter and a copy of the proposed flyer. I didn't have an email or fax for Sergio so I asked Regis to contact him and confirm if he was coming. A week later, I spoke with Sergio and he said he had the first two weeks of January off and would be honored to come. He said the flyer couldn't have been better if he'd written it himself.

Some weeks later, when I found out the plane tickets costs twice as much as I budgeted, I wrote them both back to say that I could cover their expenses but I couldn't pay them a fee. Certainly I would understand if, under those circumstances, they decided not to come. They wrote back to say it was no problem—they weren't coming for the money.

Meanwhile, Vernon had resigned as pastor of the church. I was partly relieved even though it created a whole new set of problems. I took a Breath Therapy workshop that kept me centered and clear about what really mattered to me and what didn't. Planning the workshop for Regis and Sergio was now top on my priority list and, of course manifesting the man who would lead me to my new life. Little did I know how related those two things would be.

At the beginning of November, I had another wonderful session with Michelle. I talked about my decision to leave my job at the church saying, "I'm clear about what I'm moving out of but what I'm moving into is still vague. I don't see myself working solo but as part of an organization or structure (or creating one with other people) focused on helping people move into the new millennium shift—the work of healing and transformation. I feel drawn to Peru and Regis and that kind of energy work. I'd like to find out more about the Peruvian foundation that Regis mentioned in his last letter."

A month went by and I heard nothing from Regis or Sergio. I had sent $4,000 to Peru for the airfare but still hadn't heard if their flights were confirmed or even what day they were arriving. Only four people had sent deposits for the workshop. I knew I needed at least forty to break even. At this point I was hoping for twenty. Every day I reaffirmed my trust and wrote in my journal, "I'm sure it will be fine." I'm a frugal person and just a few years before this situation would have driven me crazy with worry, but some absolute inner knowledge kept me moving forward.

The next day I heard from Sergio with a wonderful description of the workshop, the possibility of a much cheaper flight, and possible dates for their arrival and departure. I was so excited it inspired me with new ideas for promoting the workshop. Things were falling into place. I realized that trusting and believing was my best option because there was little else I could do. Two days later there was another message from Sergio saying the cheap flights were sold out and they were having trouble finding any empty seats. I wrote in my journal, "I know all that is happening is to test my new awareness and allowing me to practice behavior that assists my new wisdom."

Another week went by before I received another message from Sergio saying he had flights but didn't give me the dates or the price. Still, I felt like I was floating in a gentle, affirming flow of life. A few more people signed up for the workshop.

The following week my director from Global Ministries was in Johannesburg and I told him I wouldn't be renewing my contract. It was a lovely meeting in which he expressed interest in my Peru story and the workshop I was organizing. He encouraged me to trust my instincts as I searched for my new direction. "Well, it's done", I thought, "No going back now." I had one year for something new to materialize. Surely it would be made known to me by then.

One week until Christmas. Still no confirmation from Peru. I decided to book an auditorium in the northern suburbs for an evening lecture two days after the workshop. That would give me a better chance to recoup my expenses. One of my friends had a friend at the daily newspaper who said she'd mention it in her 'things to do' column. Great.

New Year's Eve. An article ran in the paper about the workshop, but didn't mention the lecture. Oh well, I was up to 16 bookings with the promise of a few more. Still no arrival or departure dates.

Fortunately for my disposition, the Christmas holidays in South Africa are like the 4th of July in the USA—sunny, bright, and warm, with outdoor picnics and braais (barbeques). None of that heavy cold, gray, winter energy. My spirits remained buoyant and excited. I no longer cared about the money or who would be coming. I was going to be there and that was enough for me.

Finally, on January 4th, I got an email saying they would arrive in two days at 11:40 am. The message said we would need a place with flowing water, a mountaintop and a cave for the "initiations". I wasn't sure what that meant so I decided to wait for them before launching that search. I didn't have time anyway. Last minute bookings were doubling my original list. I might just get forty after all! Regis and Sergio said that each day of the workshop would deal with one of the four elements and the corresponding sacred word. It sounded great. I couldn't wait.

It was really happening! I had manifested this workshop with these two amazing men. Talk about daring. I had even surprised myself. Maybe it's true what Regis said, "Only when the disciple is prepared, does the master appear."

I picked them up at the airport on the 6th and the roller coaster began its ascent. And what a ride it would be.

Are You Wondering?

When things aren't going well, how do you continue to have faith?

I continue to have faith because it is my faith that sustains me when things are going "wrong" or not going in the way that I would like. It is my faith that knows the divine spirit is assisting me even when it seems like everything is collapsing around me. When I first went to South Africa, I was struck by the deep faith of so many black people. Their faith was what kept them believing that justice would one day prevail and the harshness of their lives under the apartheid regime would change. In fact, it was their faith that urged them to continue resisting injustice even at great cost to themselves and their families. They expressed their faith through their actions.

I met Joe Seremane in 1990 six months after Mandela was released from prison and reform had begun. He was the director of Justice and Reconciliation at the South Africa Council of Churches. He told me the story of how he was detained by secret police in 1977 and held without charges or trail for 28 months. He was beaten and tortured nearly to death. At the moment he thought he was dying, he turned his soul over to God and heard a voice. "I have given you life and they will not take it away from you." Soon after the torture stopped. He told me how he then befriended one of his young white guards. Joe said to me, "Our God is a foolish God who asks us to do foolish things like love our enemies."

I learned from Joe that you don't really know who you are or what you believe until things start to get difficult. It is then that you draw on the resources you have developed deep within yourself. It is then that your faith really works for you.

Try This

Take advantage of your difficult experiences to discover what really matters to you, to discover who you really are and who you want to be.

Why does a person have to be ready before the master comes?

If you aren't ready then you are not open to learning what the master has to teach you. The master could come and you wouldn't be aware of it or interested in what the master had to say. Masters know this and would prefer not to waste their time and energy that could be better spent on other valuable things. There are certain experiences (like pre-requisites for university) that you need to have on your own before you can advance to higher levels. You need to develop your sensibilities and intuition. Then you will recognize when the master appears and take advantage of it.

Try This

During your meditation time, ask yourself what you most want to learn. Then listen for the answer. When you can identify what you want to learn, teachers (in many disguises) will become available to you.

To Dare

Fear is a toxic substance. It blocks your ability to function clearly. For the sake of discussion let's divide fear into two types: physical fear and emotional fear. When you are startled or in physical danger, your body produces adrenalin that is a stimulant, momentarily increasing your strength and ability to defend yourself. This is a self-produced form of protection. But even adrenalin in large doses becomes toxic to your system.

Emotional fear is toxic in other ways. It keeps you paralyzed or disabled from changing, adapting, growing, improving. It saps your energy, which could be used for more creative endeavors. If you are afraid of being hurt or afraid of being robbed, or afraid of loosing, failing, doing something wrong, looking like a fool – the list is a long one- you not only prevent positive change from happening in your life, but you are actually harming your system in a way that could eventually lead to physical illnesses like cancer and heart disease.

To dare, is to move beyond fear. Daring overcomes fear because you choose to act in a different way than you are used to acting. Each time you choose to do something that feels right to you but also a little scary, a little uncomfortable—or very scary and very uncomfortable—you are altering your patterns, not just emotionally but also bio-chemically. So each time it will get a little easier. Your system will adapt to support your more daring behavior. It will feel a little more natural to choose what you desire, even if it leads you into the unknown rather than the comfortable status quo that is no longer serving you.

Your life won't change if you don't dare to change it. Wherever you are in your life right now, there is more to be learned, more to be discovered. It is easy to settle for what you are and what you have, to convince yourself that it is enough, it's all there is. But just as your cellular body continues to replace its cells with new ones, if you don't continue to grow emotionally and spiritually you become less vital, less alive.

Part of our human nature desires sameness and familiarity. But I believe that there is a spark in each one of us, that some people might call your "soul" that wants you to discover more than what you already are and have and know. This spark calls out to you urging you to look beyond the next corner, to dig deeper into your own reserve of inner wisdom, to discover your bigger purpose for being alive on this planet at this moment in time.

In order to do that, you must learn to dare.

SECTION THREE:
TO WANT

CENTRO ESPIRITUAL UNIVERSAL INKARI

VISION:

To use the healing power of love, central to all religions and spiritual traditions, to bring about unity and peace for a new global age.

WHY PERU?

The Sacred Valley in the Andes of Peru is a place of strong spiritual energy. As people from all over the world gather here, we can harness that energy to bring about a shift in the collective consciousness of humanity by living out the truth of our unity in practical ways.

ACTIVITIES:

The Centro will be a gathering place for individuals and groups of diverse religious and spiritual traditions from around the world, for spiritual practice and social service. There will be centers on the property, such as a Conference Center; a Healing Center, an Education Center and a crafts center.

Chapter 9: Intention Is Everything

To want something is to begin the process of creating it. Intention is everything. But what we want must be free to travel its own course, rather than held so tightly by our desire that we strangle it. Like the farmer who was so anxious to assist his crops that every night he would pull on the new shoots, our efforts to push the process can actually prevent our desire from occurring. To clearly name our want is a powerful creative act. Our intention must be clear and then released with love to fly its own course, which often if not always lands us in a much better place than we thought we were headed.

In 1987, I wanted a new vocation, a job that had meaning and purpose, but also paid me a living wage. That much was clear. Would I have chosen three years in seminary getting my Masters of Divinity and then a ministry with homeless people in Johannesburg's inner city? Not from where I stood in 1987. In fact, I can recall about that time, watching a segment on 60 Minutes, about a priest in Philadelphia who worked with homeless men there. I was thoroughly disgusted by the grimy environment and depressing subject matter. I listened to the priest say how uplifting and fulfilling it was for him and how rich were his relationships with these men. I could see he was telling the truth but I just couldn't imagine how such a thing was possible. "I could NEVER do that, " I thought.

But by April 1988, my nine months of unemployed searching, had given birth to this wild notion that I wanted to go to seminary. Once at seminary, I was awakened to social injustice and global imbalance, which lead me to want to spend the summer in Africa. Then I wanted to go back to Johannesburg. By the time Vernon invited me to do the workshop at St. George's soup kitchen, I wanted to help, so I said yes (tentatively, for four weeks). Then I remembered the priest in Philadelphia and I knew exactly what he was talking about.

From there the perfect job was created for me, with meaning and purpose, a living wage, and so much more. That is the creative power of "to want".

The clearer our intention, the better, but, it is also important to know there are many layers hidden under each intention. Therefore the deeper we go with our own awareness and consciousness about what we really want and why, the better chance we have of manifesting it. Simply to want money, a job, or a car, doesn't carry the same weight of intention as clearly envisioning how those things would impact our lives and the lives that we touch. I believe our intention has more weight, more force, more power to manifest, if it has an element of purposefulness inherent in it.

Purposefulness, as I understand it, has to do with our discovery of why we are here. I don't think there is necessarily a predestined answer to why we are each here. Rather, I believe we each have a buried treasure to discover, and that our life purpose is the search for our treasure and the process of using it on a continual basis to become the best person one can be. The closer our want is to that, the stronger is the force of our intention to manifest it. But also the less likely it is to look like what we had in mind!

In January 1998, I wanted more adventure in my life. So I committed to doing two things a month beyond my comfort zone. During my first outing (the lecture on Peruvian energy healing), I wanted to know more. I wanted to go to Peru. After finding myself in the jungle, I wanted to see my future direction, where I would be and what I would be doing. "It depends on you. What do you want?" "I want to meet that man who is wise and will teach me many things, who will love me deeply." "Even if it changes everything else in your life?" "Yes, that's what I want."

After Peru, I wanted to know still more. So my teachers came to me.

Are You Wondering?

How do my efforts to push the process of getting what I want, actually prevent it from occurring? It seems like you are contradicting yourself.

By envisioning and clearly defining for yourself what you want is a very important step. It is the beginning of the creative process. Just like planting a seed. But just as a seed requires a period of gestation and unseen (underground) growth, your desire also needs time and space to manifest. There are many conditions– both helpful and adverse– that will contribute to the possibility of the seed coming to full flower. Some you can control and some you cannot. This is also true for your intention. Sometimes if you push too hard to make something happen before its time – like the farmer pulling on the new shoots to make them grow faster, your actions might have an adverse effect. You don't always know the best way to make your intention a reality but if you believe that there is a power higher than your own (divine energy) that is assisting you, then it is better to give yourself a little room for that energy to work on your behalf. Maybe there is a way you hadn't thought of that might work better than the one you are pushing to make happen. To want something is a very important part of the process but wanting something is not the same thing as forcing it into existence through the power of your will. In Spanish the word Querer means both to want and to love. Just as you love your children and want the best for them, sometimes you have to let them go out on their own to discover life for themselves.

Try This

Set your intention and let it free to grow in its own time and own way. Have faith in the process and watch expectantly for it to manifest. Take actions to promote what you want but also love it enough to let it move in its own way.

Can we manifest bad things by our intentions?

Intentions are powerful. So whatever you think about, worry about, spend time considering, you are giving those things energy – like watering a plant. When you feed your fear by giving it your time and attention, then you are helping it to manifest. So in that way, yes, you can manifest "bad" things. All the more reason to be careful what you focus on. Don't waste your energy on worry and fear. It is like throwing gasoline down the drain, instead of putting it in your car. Better to use your limited supply of fuel to take yourself where you want to go.

Try This

If you find yourself thinking about things you are afraid of happening, be conscious of that and shift your thinking. Use positive affirmations like, "I am happy". "I am healthy". "I am safe". "The divine creator is protecting me." These affirmations will remind you of the intentions you want to manifest.

Chapter 10: What Do You Want?

"All of the past year has lead me to today," I wrote in my journal, the January morning after Regis and Sergio arrived. "Having them here has already opened me and now I am ready to see, to know, to be, to become."

We talked together like old friends, and I discovered that Sergio and Regis had only met each other in June at the conference. They hadn't spoken again until Regis called him about coming to Johannesburg. How interesting that we all met each other at the same time and this was the first workshop they had taught about the Andean tradition. They had come because of me, they said.

They told me about their separate but parallel journeys of spiritual questing. Sergio had spent many years in the east, first as a young man and later for his work. In addition to the Andean tradition, which they both had spent thirty years mastering, Sergio had also studied Chi Kung, Tai Chi, Feng Shui and Reiki. Throughout his travels, masters of many spiritual traditions recognized him and shared their healing techniques and special teachings with him. All of his life, he knew that he had been called to bring about transformation and committed himself to this cause. When he became a master in the Andean tradition he was given the Quechua name, *Hatun Runa*.

Regis spoke of his last level of training ten years before, where his ability "to see" and heal energetically, had been fully awakened. He had climbed one of Cusco's snow capped mountains with his master, who then left him alone camped at 17, 000 ft. for a three-day vision quest. When Regis returned to Cusco, he could see every aspect of each person's life— past, present, and future. It was a wild cacophony that he couldn't turn off. He knew more than was helpful for him or the others. He again climbed the mountain and when he returned the following day, his normal vision had been restored, but he was left with the ability to access that other vision, in order to assist the healing and transformation of others and himself. He was given the Quechua name *Kamaq Weageq*.

We talked for six or eight hours that first day. Within the joy and elation of what they shared with me, I felt intense longing, and I told them I wanted to "see" like they see. They said I would but I needed to take it one step at a time. During dinner I told them how I became a minister in South Africa and how I was ready to move to the next step. I asked them to tell me what I would be doing next and where. They laughed at my impatience and said we would talk more about that when the workshop was over.

We talked late into the night. I felt so full, so rich, so open, so excited. I slept only four hours and woke at dawn full of energy. The three of us went to buy candles, wine, charcoal and other things needed for rituals during the workshop. I took care of last minute registrations, packed the car and we were on our way. We had two hours before people started arriving for the workshop to scout the area for the river, the cave and the mountain we would use later. Everything fell into place, as if I'd known what they would need. They were very pleased with the venue I'd chosen. Good Feng Shui, Sergio said.

Thozi, my dear friend who worked with me in the outreach ministry and was attending the workshop, took over the registration of people as they arrived, which gave me time to help Regis and Sergio prepare for everything. The first session started after we all had dinner together.

Kamaq Weageq (Regis) spoke first and explained how each day we would discuss one of the four elements. We were starting with Earth, to give thanks to our mother, who gives us life. He spoke about the importance of connecting with the mountains and rivers and giving thanks to all the elements. He spoke about the power of love.

Hatun Runa (Sergio) then described the chakana, the Andean cross with its four equal sides and center circle of power.

The South is Fire, which sanctifies and transmutes us, burns away the old so the new can emerge from the embers. The corresponding word is to Dare. The West is Earth, which cleanses our heavy energy, *hoocha*, and transforms it into refined energy, *sami,* in the same way fertilizer nourishes soil to bring forth new growth. The corresponding word is to Want. The North is Air, which purifies and enlightens us so we can expand our sense of time and space. It is the place of wisdom and deep knowledge. The corresponding word is to Know. The East is Water, which washes and balances us. Similar to the Earth, Water can receive all our fears and frustrations and wash them away. The corresponding word is to Be Silent.

The opening session concluded with a despacho ceremony for *pachamama* (mother earth). The ritual of making a despacho is like a communal prayer. Only second level priests (or higher) can perform them. This one lasted about an hour. Watching it was like a group meditation. They put a square piece of paper on the floor and carefully placed many elements on the paper in a ritual manner, including flowers, seeds, grains and candies. Coca leaves, a sacred plant to the Inkas (and Andean people throughout the ages), were placed carefully in the despacho, each representing a special prayer. We were each given a coca leaf in which we were invited to "put" our request. These too were placed into the despacho.

The bundle was then folded and tied shut. Each of us came forward to be "cleansed" by the bundle. Sergio had wrapped the bundle in a manta of Andean woven cloth. We each stood before him as he held the square bundle with both hands and passed it from our heads, down each arm, leg, front and back. Then we moved to Regis who was standing in a similar fashion, holding his *mesa* (a manta-wrapped bundle containing his power elements, including stones and other objects from special places were he had been initiated). He passed his *mesa* over us in a similar fashion but whereas the despacho was removing our heavy energy, Regis' *mesa* was empowering us with its refined energy.

When the session was over, we all went outside in the moon-lit night and buried the despacho, as a gift for mother earth, asking for her blessing on our time together. After the ceremony, I went back to the room Regis and Sergio were sharing in order to discuss how things had gone. Within the few hours, we had moved from being forty strangers from different parts of the city and the world, to a group inspired by what we heard and excited by the possibilities of what the weekend would bring. I was amazed to see the shift in energy that Regis and Sergio had created within the group in such a short time.

The next morning Sergio spoke about the element of water and the sacred word: to Be Silent. He said we were really "bags of water" because so much of our physical makeup is water. Because of this fact, it was important for us to work consciously with this element, to befriend it and learn from it.

Regis then spoke about the "priesthood" of the Andean tradition and the levels of training involved. Because the Andean tradition is not a religion, "priesthood" may be a misleading term. Andean priests, he told us, are thought of as healers and spiritual teachers. The four levels of mastery are called in Quechua: *paqo* (simply meaning priest), *pampa misayoq*, *alto misayoq*, and *kuraq akulleq*. He explained that there are three sub levels of *alto misayoq* and that very few people have reached the level of *kuraq akulleq*, which takes many years of training and experience.

After the discussions, they made a despacho for *unu* (the Quechua word for water). Similar to the one we had done the night before for Earth, it contained some elements that were different. Regis used it to cleanse us and Sergio empowered us with his mesa. The despacho was then placed on an altar with candles and both of their mesas, where it would stay until burned at the end of the workshop with other despachos we would make for Air and Fire.

After lunch we drove to a nearby river. I followed Regis into the rocky, knee-deep, swiftly flowing water, as the rest of the group followed. We held hands to steady ourselves. Regis then invited us to shut our eyes and feel the water flowing over our skin, and to release all our concerns, fears and frustrations. It was a soothing, liberating feeling. Later we sat on the bank of the river and did a meditation with our eyes open, semi-focused on the flowing river, releasing our cares into the steady stream.

We returned to the conference center to do exercises with the Earth, where we embraced a tree and listened for what it had to teach us. In the next exercise, we lay belly down on the ground, to converse with our loving mother. We were invited to give her all our heavy energy, our anxieties and frustrations (our 'shit') that she lovingly receives as fertilizer to enrich her soil. In this exchange there is life-giving reciprocity.

After dinner, we had a fire outside under the stars. We passed a stone from one person to the next as we shared some of what each of us had been feeling, experiencing, and discovering. Many people spoke of their strong connection with the water or the earth in the exercises we had done, some recalling tearfully how as children they knew this connection but had forgotten it. Others spoke of their profound gratitude to Regis and Sergio for coming such a long way to share these teachings with us. More than anything, that's what I felt, a profound gratitude.

Saturday morning, during our first session, we began to learn the Inka cosmology and prophecies. Regis told us we were lucky to be alive at such an auspicious time, when the ancient prophecies would be manifesting. In 1986, a 25-year transition period had begun, a time of great spiritual awakening around the world. Many people would be drawn to the strong spiritual energy of Peru, for the axis of spiritual power that had been centered in the Himalayas, had now shifted to the Andes.

The Inka prophecies spoke of the coming of a new age of prosperity and abundance, of global unity, peace and love, called the "*taripay pacha*", meaning the age of meeting ourselves again. Between 2006-2012, a new, fifth level of "Inka priests" would emerge, who could heal with a touch and would have many extraordinary powers. Regis said there would be a council of twelve, six men and six women, who would be spiritual and political leaders of a new kind. They would usher in an even higher, sixth level of universal consciousness. These people, he told us, could be from anywhere, not just Peru.

A chill ran through my spine as I listened intently. I felt such a strong connection to what he was saying, as if a part of my being had known this information before. He said that we were all here in this moment, along with many others all over the world, who were working with the forces of light and love, to raise our human collective consciousness to bring about this shift.

"*Pero…*", he said in Spanish, with his delightful elfin smile, "*siempre pero…*" But, always but… there was lots of work to be done! We must learn to let go of our fear and trust in the power of unconditional love. We must learn to connect with the elements and give thanks often to *Pachamama* (mother earth), *Tahita Inti* (father sun) and *Wiracocha* (creator/spirit). We must work ("*llankay*"), learn wisdom ("*yachay*") and love ("*munay*").

A fundamental principal in the Andean tradition of the Inkas, he taught us, is "*anyi*" or reciprocity. This meant the leaders, political and spiritual, were obligated (as he was teaching us to be) to share their knowledge, rather than use it for their own personal power, as happens so often today. This was our challenge, to change the patterns of the past in order to bring about the long awaited *taripay pacha*.

We then watched them make another despacho, this time as an offering to the Air. As before, we were each given a coca leaf in which we were invited to "put" our request. My prayer was to be able to do my part in bringing about this new age of peace and unity.

As with the other times, Regis folded the bundle and each of us came forward to be cleansed by the despacho and then moved to Sergio to be empowered by his *mesa*. I could feel the energy of the despacho and the *mesa* as they passed over my body.

It was a powerful morning. My head was spinning with thoughts and emotions. But there were logistical things that needed attending to and I was soon back in the everyday world of pressures and distractions. The afternoon outing needed to be organized. After lunch we drove in several cars to a Nature Reserve about 30 minutes away, to work with the element of Air.

The Nature Reserve was rugged and remote. We climbed up a hill until we reached some rocks that looked down on a beautiful green valley. There was not a breath of wind when we arrived. The air was still. Then Regis and Sergio did a ceremony invoking the spirit of the four directions. When they summoned the wind, as if on cue, a gust began to blow with such force, that we were all totally amazed. We did a standing meditation with the wind. I felt like I could fly. It was an incredible feeling. We then did an exercise where we looked at the air with loosened focus and were able to see small elements in the air, dancing sparkles that delighted and mesmerized us.

Next, we lay belly-down on one of the rocks. The mountains in this part of South Africa are said to be more than 32,000,000 years old. We were asked to listen to these ancient elders and hear what they had to teach us. The sun had been shining when we arrived on the mountain so the stone I lay on was warm. But the cool wind was still blowing and just as we lay down, it began to rain slightly. When the meditation was over it was still overcast and blustery, but directly above us there was a circular opening in the clouds. It was unbelievable but true, a small round patch of blue sky directly over us. Just then the sun broke through and slowly, as we packed our things to hike down the mountain, the clouds came back together. I was in awe of the power of these men to work with the elements. It wouldn't be the last time I saw them change the weather.

That night we all sat around a blazing campfire to ask questions and receive answers. I was quiet, listening to everyone's heartfelt longings to know. I watched the flames dance around the fire that warmed us, as we sat on logs under the chilly Johannesburg summer night. By the end, I felt present and open to whatever life had in store for me.

Sergio came up to me afterwards, looked directly into my soul and asked me, "What do you want? If you want this spiritual path then you must be clear and choose it. Then you can also have everything else you want. But if you focus on the mundane things of life and get stuck in your emotions, then that's where you will stay, which is fine, if that is what you want. You need to choose."

"I want this spiritual path." I answered.

"Then don't let your emotions rule you. You must learn to stay focused on what matters." He told me that all his powers come from the divine source and that learning to access those powers requires discipline and practice. He described a time he was asked to speak with a group of foreigners about the Andean tradition. He called on divine inspiration and ended up speaking in a language that he didn't even know. He said I must trust that I will be given what I need.

I understood what he meant, that if I focused on my highest good, I could have everything else also. I knew from my own experience that when I was open and connected with God, the universe was free to assist me with all that I needed. In fact, I was experiencing it right then. These two amazing men had come all the way from Peru to South Africa to teach me.

That night I went to bed determined to recognize and accept my calling to this new level of my spiritual path. We woke up at 4:30 for a sunrise "Inti Rami" ceremony. Blurry eyed, I was out on the lawn by 5am. Regis was there waiting for me with an antique woven poncho. Regis and Sergio wore similar ponchos for all the despachos and other sacred ceremonies. He had brought this old and very special one for me, all the way from Peru. He told me to put it on because I was leading the procession and doing the opening invocation. For a brief moment I panicked and thought, "I can't do that. I don't know how." Then I remembered the story Sergio told me the night before about being given the words. A calm assurance came over me and I knew I could, with God's help.

Every morning so far had been cloudy but this day the sky was clear and the sun broke the horizon in the most awesome ball of orange and fuchsia that I have ever seen. I stood on a small grassy hill facing due east with Regis and Sergio in their ponchos on either side of me and the rest of the group gathered below and behind us. As the sun rose, I raised the basket of fruit I was holding toward the sky and spoke the invocation to *Tahita Inti* in such a strong, loud voice that even they were surprised. I don't remember what I said because the words had not come from my thoughts but from a higher source. We stood for a long time in silence watching the glowing ball of fire become full and round and light up the sky in shades of golden pink. We had been told that the energy from the sun could be accessed most powerfully at sunrise. Soon the sun had risen too far above the horizon to look at directly any longer. But the energy I had felt and received was very strong and palpable.

After breakfast Sergio spoke about Fire and the sacred word to Dare. Then he and Regis made a despacho for the fire, where we used the yellow sunflowers we had gathered from the side of the road coming back from our trip the day before. This despacho was especially beautiful. In the afternoon we did some more practical exercises and then prepared the fire to burn all three remaining despachos. Regis and Sergio asked me to wear my poncho and carry the despachos as we processed out to the fire for the closing ceremony. I felt simultaneously thrilled and inadequate to have been given such an honored place, but I remembered my intention to claim my calling and received the opportunity graciously.

After the burning of the despachos, we went back in the meeting room and each person was given a chance to say what the workshop had meant to them. Regis and Sergio had me sit with them in the front facing everyone. I was moved to tears many times, to hear people share how they had been awakened, transformed and inspired. Many people spoke of visions and messages they had seen and received during different exercises and meditations. It was clear that everyone present had experienced a powerful shift within themselves. The room was vibrating with love and peace.

When everyone finished it was my turn to share. Tears were streaming down my face when Regis and Sergio had said how much courage and faith it had taken for me to arrange this workshop, without knowing anything. They said again they had come because of me. "It was easy for me to organize the workshop," I said, "once I decided that I wanted them to come. The hard part for me is always *after* I take the leap of daring, not before." I told the group that during parts of the workshop, I struggled to stay focused but Regis and Sergio always helped me to find my center again. Because of that I was able to recognize my calling and commit myself to this spiritual path and that I had no words to thank them enough.

After dinner, we closed the workshop by dancing to Andean music with lots of hugs and kisses all around. I couldn't help thinking what a difference there was in the energy of the group from when we started only four nights before. Who were these Peruvian master shamans? Had they really come because of me? What else was still in store for me, I wondered.

Are You Wondering?

What if I want many things and some of them are conflicting?
If two things you want are in direct conflict with each other, then you have to choose which one you want more. Be careful though, that you don't get stuck in your emotions, torn between one thing and another. You will just get exhausted from the battle and have no energy left to identify clearly what you really want (like I was doing during the workshop). When you get stuck in your emotions, it is usually because the ego is speaking louder than your inner wisdom. The ego will often lead you down the wrong path because it is more interested in comfort than it is in growth or change. To manifest a new vision, a daring vision, involves risk. The ego doesn't like to loose so sometimes that part of yourself will seem in conflict with what you want.

Try This
When you feel conflicted, take time to refocus, to go deep within yourself. Imagine that you are surrounded by a bright white light, the light of Divine love. Breathe deeply, in and out, for at least 10 minutes. This will calm you and help you access your inner wisdom. Then you will have greater clarity; clarity to choose what you really want.

Can you tell us more about the purpose of despachos?

A despacho is an ancient Andean ritual. It is an offering, a gift to the elements or the apus. A gift to the divine creator who provides for all our needs. In this offering is the equally ancient principle of anyi, a Quechua word which means reciprocity or exchange. It means 'as we give we receive and as we receive, we give'. The despacho is performed by an Andean master who becomes the mediator between the people and Divine Creator (Wirachocha), much like a priest saying mass or a rabbi leading a temple service. It is a ceremony of thanksgiving. There are despachos performed for all important occasions such as a new business or building project, the birth of a child, an engagement, moving into a new house, any occasion where one wants a blessing or wants to give thanks. The person performing the ceremony, as well as the assistant, kneels on the ground. There is a square piece of paper in front of them and many elements that are placed on the paper in a ritual fashion. The master blows on each element with intention and thanksgiving. The elements (seeds, incense, flowers, coca leaves, herbs, candies, etc.) represent all elements of our lives and also the three levels of existence (hanaq pacha, kay pacha and uku pacha). It is a powerful ceremony that really needs to be experienced rather than explained in words. Like most rituals, it summons the power of the spirit and becomes more than the sum of its parts.

Chapter 11: The Power of the Elements

There was a great deal of interest from many of the participants, including myself, in learning more. On the last day of the workshop, Regis and Sergio indicated that they were willing to do a first level initiation with us if there were at least ten people. Twenty-three people signed the list. They told me later that it was their intention when they came, to initiate me to the first level, if that was what I wanted. They felt I was ready.

The day that Regis had explained the levels of the "Andean priesthood", I had asked him what level he and Sergio were. He told me in his quiet humble manner that they were both Kuraq Akulleqs (the fourth and highest existing level). Although Alto Misayoqs have the power to initiate others into the tradition, I knew it was a great honor that we would be initiated by such high-level masters.

They informed us that the first level was a stage where paqos learned to work in deeper relation with the elements. The initiation was an energetic opening, an awakening of our potential to connect with the elements in a more profound way. However, it was up to us and our intentional practice, whether this awakening would develop within us or not.

Theresa, one of the workshop participants, invited us to use her farm for the initiation. It was about an hour's drive north of the city and was situated adjacent to a sacred (and very old) mountain in the Magaliesberg range, with a river nearby and a cave —all elements that Regis and Sergio said they needed for our sacred ceremonial work together. We agreed to meet there at 8am in two days time. We were told to abstain from eating from the night before and to bring fruit with us to break the fast at the end of the day.

In addition to making plans and preparations for the initiation on Wednesday, I was also fielding phone calls all day Monday. Over the weekend, an article had mysteriously appeared in the Sunday paper about the public talk I had organized for Wednesday night. The paper had put my phone number in the article but not the time or address of the talk. After returning all the calls left over the weekend, the phone continued to ring with barely a pause between calls. I finally put all the information on the answering machine and told people to just come without reservations. I laughed because now I was assured of recouping all my expenses. It also looked like we would have enough money left over to go to a nearby Game Reserve for a few days of relaxation after the initiation and before Regis and Sergio flew back to Peru.

On Tuesday I had to work at the church's drop-in center. I asked Regis and Sergio to lead the Healing Workshop that I regularly ran on Tuesday mornings. Regis led the guided meditation and Sergio translated it into English. Afterwards, Regis went around the circle and spoke to each person directly about the issues with which he could see they were dealing, just as he had done with John and others in Urubamba. There were about twelve people in the circle. Some I knew well but others I did not. It was clear that Regis knew exactly what was troubling each person and gave them simple but meaningful advice. They were stunned, as was I, that this man who didn't even speak a language they could understand, was so clearly able to see them—their true inner selves—and offer healing, transforming alternatives with such love, such unconditional love and encouragement.

Will I ever have such vision, grace and knowledge to use in the work of healing, I wondered. I hoped the next day's initiation would be a significant step toward that goal.

Many things were needed to prepare for the initiation. Simon, our translator at the workshop, had a sister from Bolivia who had traditional Andean cloth which we needed for each person's mesa. But the cloth had to be cut and sewn. We needed more elements for the despacho and each person's mesa. I was learning how much easier it was to trust that all the elements would be provided in time, than it was to fret, worry and think that it just wasn't possible. I was beginning to understand the power of intention. I was up very late with Regis and Sergio that night making all the final preparations. And up again at dawn with only a few hours sleep, full of excitement and some trepidation.

It was an extraordinarily beautiful day, sunny and clear. After we all assembled at Theresa's, we hiked in silence for about forty minutes to the top of the grassy mountain where we could see rolling hills around us, the valley below and open blue sky above. We did the first ceremony there, making a despacho for the Air and spending time in quiet meditation. We were told to keep silent the whole day, unless they asked us a direct question.

After our work with the Air was complete and the despacho ceremony finished, we hiked down the mountain and halfway up again along another path to a large, ancient cave. We sat outside and waited as each person was blind-folded and taken into the cave by Regis and Sergio, one on either side, walking us backwards into the heart and womb of Pachamama (Mother Earth). The cave was deep, dark and cool. I stumbled over stones, as I was guided backwards, but I felt safe in the trusted arms of my teachers. When we were all inside the cave, sitting on various rocks, Regis led a beautiful guided meditation, which gave me insight into my purpose for being alive at this time; to be a healer and an instrument of transformation. I had seen that this was the commitment I had made before I was born. I knew that this initiation was reconnecting me in a strong energetic way to that calling and I felt such peace and gratitude.

It seemed to me that we each emerged from that cave with a new sense of ourselves, visible on our faces and in the auras that glowed around us. We continued in silence as we walked down to the river. We each found a spot on its rocky tree-lined, muddy banks, to sit on the ground with our feet in the chilly, flowing water. As we sat with our eyes closed in silent meditation, Regis and Sergio came to each of us and sprinkled water from the river onto our heads in a type of baptism, to connect us more deeply with the element of water.

Then we walked back up to the opening of the cave where we prepared the fire and where each of our colorful mantas laid on the ground waiting to be filled and folded into what would become our "mesa" medicine bundle. Regis and Sergio then called us each by name and we went over to receive our mesa. Each one held three elements that they gave to us. We were invited to place our own sacred stones and elements into our mesa, in a ritual prayerful manner that they taught us. We were also told not to open our mesa in the presence of people who had not been initiated, that the inside of our mesas could only be seen by people of the same level or higher. As I understood it, this had to do with keeping the energy of these sacred elements protected so their power (our power) would remain strong and pure.

Once we each had our mesa, we were called again, one at a time. I was the first. I stood before them with my mesa over my heart center, held by my crossed arms. Sergio put his mesa on top of my chest and arms while Regis stood behind me with his mesa on my back. They spoke simple words of dedication. Then through their hands and mesas they energetically transmitted to me the ancient karpay (power) given to them by their masters handed down through the ages, ordaining me a paqo. I felt full of awe and wonder by my entry into this ancient tradition. This process was repeated with the other 22 initiates. Now it was up to us, to use this sacred power for our own transformation as well as the raising of communal consciousness.

We then lit the fire to burn the despacho we had made that morning. Afterwards we laughed and cried and hugged each other and shared the fruit we had brought to break the fast. We had been eight hours together on that sacred mountain, con-necting with the elements, the earth, the air, the cave, the sun, the water. We also connected each with our own soul through the power and love of our teachers and their teachers before them. It was an extraordinary feeling.

I was a bit shocked to learn it was already 5 o'clock. Regis was giving a lecture that night at 7:00 P.M. and we were more than an hour away. Plus, we had to go back to my house to shower and change before heading back up north to the library auditorium. Shamans or no shamans, this would be a challenge, but one I was much more prepared to handle than only a few days before. We packed our things and hiked the twenty minutes back to the car. I felt light and strong at the same time, confident it would all work out somehow.

When we got back to my house, my friend Fiona called from the auditorium. A hundred people were waiting. Why wasn't I there, she wanted to know. I said we would be there as soon as we could and asked if she could have the guard open the door and would she mind collecting the money for me. I thanked God she was there and able to handle the situation.

By the time we arrived, there was standing room only—160 rather agitated people. Regis was giving the talk but we needed Simon to translate and Simon still hadn't arrived. I went to the front of the crowd and told them that we were waiting for our translator who we hoped would arrive shortly. Then someone asked me who I was. I smiled, a bit surprised by the question, and words began to flow freely from my mouth. I explained the work I was doing with homeless people in Johannesburg for the past eight years, and how it led to my interest in alternative healing, which eventually led me to Peru where I met Regis and discovered his extraordinary gifts for vision and healing.

I soon became aware that the agitated energy in the auditorium had shifted into a calm, attentive silence. I was delighted by the effortless ease with which the words flowed from me. I felt a surprising sense of love and compassion for the group and for the people about whom I was speaking. I knew I was communicating beyond my words the love and peace and gratitude I was experiencing. I was also aware of a tangible force that was flowing through the crowd like a vapor people were breathing in. It was transforming their disposition. I knew the power I felt was not something I possessed but rather something that was flowing through me from a higher source. I knew it was directly related to the work we had done earlier in the day. It was the divine connectedness I had experienced during the initiation.

Soon Simon arrived and the lecture began. Simultaneous translation is not an easy task and combined with the fact that neither Simon nor Regis had much experience speaking in front of large crowds, it took a while for the conversation to flow. I could sense a bit of restlessness in the audience. I wanted them to experience the power of Regis and the Andean tradition and I began to feel a desire to step in, to take control. Not so much in a literal sense, but I started to feel distracted and uncomfortable. The effortless flow of transforming energy I had felt earlier had vanished into thin air. During the question and answer period, Simon and Regis, asked me to call on the people. As the agitation of the crowd grew, so did my desire for control. The sensation I felt was now the polar opposite of before and I could see it manifesting in the mood of the crowd. But I just wasn't able to shift it. The more I sought control, the more out of control I felt.

I got into a power struggle with a woman who was giving a speech of her own rather than asking a question. The crowd was also jeering at her. I felt stuck between a rock and a hard place and lost my cool by raising my voice in an ironic effort to silence everyone. Not my finest hour. Regis, on the other hand, was calm and relaxed, shifting the situation in his own gentle loving way, side-stepping the negative energy, waiting for it to dissipate while I rushed head-strong into it unprotected and therefore powerless to transform it.

In hindsight I can clearly see the dynamic but at the time I was simply stuck. Regis answered the woman in a diplomatic fashion and befriended her in the process (thereby disarming her). We took a few more questions and then I thanked everyone for coming. I breathed a sigh of relief but couldn't really relax because many people were coming up to me all at once. I couldn't believe I had moved from such a state of bliss to inner torment in such a short time. My head was spinning with circuit overload. I was hungry and I just wanted to leave.

Regis and Sergio, however, were calmly and delightfully answering questions and saying their good-byes to many of the workshop participants who attended the lecture. When we finally left, I got lost driving to a restaurant in my neighborhood, which I had been to many times. I was angry with myself because I had lost my center and was begging them to explain to me 'WHY do I always do that' and get stuck.

They just told me to forget about it, which only made me more frustrated. It was a classic case of getting stuck in my emotions and they were keeping distant from the fray rather than fueling the fire. How do you get unstuck from your emotions, I genuinely longed to know. The answer I kept getting was "it doesn't matter," "akuna mathata," "let it go." It has taken me many months to learn that getting unstuck from one's emotions actually is a matter of simply letting go, but like most simple truths it's a complex process and takes continuous practice as well as clear desire. Most of us like our emotions too much to let go of them easily because they make us feel "alive". They've become habit-forming. But the truth of the matter is that anger, frustration, guilt, shame (all "control" emotions) are toxic to our systems. Holding on to them keeps us feeling out of control and also cuts off our access to divine love, which is what heals, soothes and restores our inner peace.

At that moment however, I hadn't yet learned these lessons very well. I still thought that giving time and attention to my anger/guilt/shame would better allow it to burn out in its own time. And if I "understood" what triggered it, then I could prevent it from happening again. Fortunately, it was hard to stay angry in the presence of their loving energy. Soon I calmed down and was able to let go. I imagine on some level it was all a part of my initiation. And what a day it had been! The opportunities to learn and grow were coming fast and furiously. Be careful what you ask for, I thought to myself. And I still had three more days with them!

Are You Wondering?

What does it mean to be initiated into the Andean Tradition?

There are certain traditions or organizations you can join by signing up and becoming a member. There are others where you go to school to acquire a degree or certificate that says you are qualified to perform particular activities. In the Andean spiritual tradition, like Reiki and other healing and indigenous traditions, people are trained in practices of that tradition but they also must go though certain rites of passage—an initiation—before they become active in that tradition. The initiation into Andean Spirituality has six levels, or six initiations. Before each one there are new teachings and healing techniques that must be learned and mastered. As part of each initiation, there is an energy transmission that is passed from the master to the initiate. It is a significant and powerful part of the initiation passed down from the ancient masters to the current ones. But as Regis and Sergio reminded us, this energetic opening received by each of us, needs to be used for the raising of our own consciousness and the expansion of humanity's collective consciousness. If not, the power of this energetic opening will eventually close and become unavailable to us.

Why were you able to connect so well with the people in the auditorium before Regis' talk and not at the end?

When I first started talking to the crowd, I wasn't trying to "control" them. In fact, I did not have any intention of talking with them beyond saying that we were waiting for the translator to arrive. When someone asked me who I was and how I was connected with the Peruvian shaman, I just began to speak. I was centered and present and open to the possibility of connecting with the people who were there. The words flowed out of me, out of that centered place in me. I felt the energy I had received in my initiation and it was allowing me to speak from a loving place and relate to the people without judgment or vested interest.

Conversely, when I was calling on people to ask their questions, I was much more "task-oriented". I wanted to control the situation so it wouldn't get out of hand and I was manifesting my worst expectations. Love showed itself once again as a more powerful tool than anger when Regis intervened, not by trying to silence the woman but by engaging her with warmth and affection. Trying to control other people is always a bad idea.

Try This

Whenever you notice the urge to control someone or a situation arising, pause and look within yourself. Release your desire for "control" by stepping out of the situation (even briefly), take a few breaths, relax. Recognize that trying to control others is only making things worse. Consult your inner wisdom for an alternative solution. Remember that your own behavior is really the only behavior you have power to change.

Chapter 12: Seeing and Knowing

Following the initiation was another non-stop day of activities. Keeping up with these two had become somewhat of a marathon challenge but most of the time it was a great joy. The three of us packed camping gear and food for our overnight stay in the Pilanesberg Game Reserve, a few hours' drive northwest. In between, I was fielding phone calls and taking care of banking and accounting things from the workshop. A reporter then arrived at the house to interview Regis. Sergio translated. It was very interesting to hear a recap of the Andean philosophy and other fascinating antidotes prompted by the reporter's questions. She was as charmed and intrigued as others had been by what they had to say.

Once again I marveled that these two amazing men were sitting with me in my living room. A few nights before at dinner they were telling me how much they liked my openness and strength. They said we made a great team. I responded incredulously, "I don't know what I did to deserve being on such a team but I sure am glad to be!"

We had made arrangements to meet some people for lunch in my least favorite northern suburb, which fortunately was also in the same general direction as the Game Reserve. But of course I got lost getting there. I had basically recovered from my trauma of the night before but I was still feeling unsettled and handling lots of logistical things under a time pressure was not helping. I moved in and out of relaxed enjoyment with perplexing regularity; one minute playfully joking with them and the next feeling pressured and anxious.

We left the house late and ran into unexpected traffic, even before I got lost. Sergio was in the front seat with me, reminding me to relax. Once I asked him to clear the traffic for me and watched him make some symbols with his hands and soon thereafter the bumper-to-bumper slow-moving traffic began to loosen up. But like my moods, the congestion returned. By the time we found the restaurant, we were more than an hour late. Fortunately, everyone was still there, although nearly finished eating. Since most of the conversation was in Spanish, I felt a slight reprieve from the pressure, as I made small talk with the other person at the table who didn't speak Spanish.

An hour or so later we were back on the road. Sergio was driving and I was navigating, happy to be in the passenger seat. I gave him what I thought were clear instructions about the upcoming turn-off and dozed a little (having been sleep-deprived for many days running). I was stunned when I realized Sergio was driving past the turn-off and started screaming at him, quite literally, angrily screaming. The look on his face shocked me back into reality. It was simple enough to turn around and get back on the correct road, he reminded me. Why had I reacted so strongly? Part of me wanted to make it his fault. Hadn't I told him three times where to turn? (I realize now it was the kind of unhelpful argument that happened often with my family. But this time the dynamic had nowhere to go since Sergio wouldn't engage.) The truth was, I was thoroughly embarrassed. After apologizing, I sat in silence chastising myself.

The mood in the car lightened with time but I still felt somewhat vulnerable. Once we arrived at the check-in gate of the Game Reserve, we decided to get two tents even though they were large enough to fit three beds. Regis said he wanted his own tent. Sergio and I agreed to share the other. The bush-camp where we were staying had permanent army tents with two reasonably comfortable plank beds. It was a favorite get-away place for me on my weekends off, so I'd been there many times. The camp was a thirty minute slow drive through the park and we needed to be inside before the sun set. As with most game parks in Africa, the animals live in the open and the human guests are confined to their cars or inside a fenced-in area for sleeping.

I took over the driving. I told them that the road near the entrance rarely had animals nearby but they should look just in case. Seeing wild animals had lost its excitement for me. I was rather looking forward to spending time in the bush-camp itself, surrounded by the mountainous scenery and nearby lake, cooking over a campfire and sitting under the nighttime stars. Driving for hours on dusty roads at five miles per hour hoping to see animals wasn't really my idea of fun. So when Regis said something in Spanish from the backseat and Sergio told me that he'd seen an elephant, I presumed he was joking and kept driving. Some confusion then ensued and I reluctantly put the car in reverse, still not really believing there could be an elephant so close to the entrance.

Once again I was totally embarrassed when I saw the elephant, bigger than life, standing a few feet from the side of the road. Sergio explained to me in English that Regis was concerned that I would question him not only in this instance but several times that day. Didn't I trust him as a teacher, as a master? I tried to explain that I had misunderstood, that I thought they were teasing me, but deep down inside I knew he was right. I hadn't believed him. But why, I thought. Why hadn't I believed him? Was I doubting their power, doubting what they were teaching me, doubting that I might be able to reach their level of awareness one day if I dedicated myself to that end? I didn't know it at the time, but I was doing what many of us do after we connect with divine grace and begin to transform our lives: our fragile ego grabs back our old crutches in the form of doubts and fears in an effort to keep us right where we were, right where we're comfortable in the realm of the familiar. That's one of the reasons substantive change is so hard to manage and maintain.

At the time however, I was aware only that I felt horrible for doubting Regis and yelling at Sergio, these amazing teachers of mine who had come all the way from Peru on their vacation time, without being paid, to teach me what they knew. If I could have run away right then, I would have. But I couldn't leave the car and we still had quite a distance to drive before reaching the camp. I felt trapped both physically and emotionally. I was sure after this they would realize they had made a big mistake and kick me off their "team". I was sure I'd blown it.

They, on the other hand, had said their piece and were back to looking for animals, seeming no worse for the wear. I can't tell you if we saw anything else because I was stuck in a hell of my own making that had no windows. We finally made it to the camp at dusk and unpacked the car. I wandered off on my own thinking I was looking for kindling for our campfire but I really just needed to get away. I sat down on a rock and looked up at the darkening sky and begged for some help. Maybe I really wasn't up to the challenge. Maybe God had picked the wrong person for this job. How could I heal and transform anything if I couldn't even manage myself. I cried, which actually helped me let go of the unbearable weight of my self-criticism. Eventually I wandered back to the campsite into the loving care of Regis and Sergio.

Where had I been, they wondered and why was I so upset? I told them how bad I felt about my earlier behavior and they laughed it off. "Forget about it", they said. "It doesn't matter. If we're not upset about it, why should you be? We're the masters remember? Learn from what happened and let it go." Their confidence in me in the face of all my mistakes was very healing and reassuring. However, the real choice was up to me. If I wanted to accept this calling then I had to keep reminding myself that and rise to the occasion, not get stuck in self-pity and self-criticism, neither of which are the least bit helpful.

Regis built a fire and we cooked some vegetables. Soon after dinner, we went to bed. I for one, was exhausted. I fell asleep easily. Then, sometime in the middle of the night, I was awakened by a strong surge of energy that ran through my body. It seemed to be coming from Sergio's side of the tent. It felt like an earthquake only inside my body, starting at my heart-center. It was very strong and unlike anything I had ever felt before.

I turned to Sergio, who had been sleeping and said, "What was that?!" In his half-groggy state, he said, "Love." At first I thought it was something he had done but he said he hadn't felt anything or done anything. Too tired to make sense of it then, I went back to sleep but the energy surge happened again. In fact, it happened many times, some stronger than others. I kept asking Sergio to tell me what it was. He said only, "You know." After the second or third time, I began talking with the energy force. It said to me, "You have been chosen. You must decide what you want." I answered, with some trepidation, "Yes, I accept." It said, "If I have chosen you, who are you to doubt it?"

The surges continued through the night. The last one was so strong that I shot upright in the bed with my back arched. It was like the force of an orgasm only stronger and not sexual, I grabbed Sergio because I thought I was going mad. He kept encouraging me to interpret it and accept it for myself. "Energy and power are transmitted to us in many ways", he said. When he told Regis about it in the morning, Regis seemed pleased but didn't offer me any explanation. They suggested I take a stone from nearby to put in my mesa as a way of honoring the power of the experience.

We had breakfast, packed up and then drove for the rest of the day through the Reserve looking for animals and enjoying the scenery. I was tired since I hadn't slept much. I was unusually quiet most of the day. Late in the afternoon, as we watched a huge eagle take flight, they asked me what I had learned, what I thought of the ten days we had spent together. I paused and then answered without really thinking, "I see now and know without doubt." Then my mind, having heard what I just said added, "But I don't know what it all means or how I will get there." Regis shook his head and said, "You have said everything and nothing. Which is it? Do you see or don't you see?"

In the secret recesses of my being I knew, or rather had been reminded, that I had chosen (and been chosen) to be a healer and transformer at this wonderful time in history, to help bring about the taripay pacha described in the Inka prophecies. Saying it out loud however, in front of other people was still difficult for me. What if I was deluding myself. I would have preferred for them to tell me, just so I could be sure.

The point I realize now, that I didn't then, was that no one can give you what you are not willing to claim yourself. The challenge however, is to learn the difference between the false bravado kind of claiming that our society perpetuates, and claiming something from a true heart-centered place. The later opens the channels of energy to flow in a reciprocal give and take, allowing us to honor our gifts and use them well. The false bravado kind of claiming either makes us grab and hold things in such a stingy way that they benefit no one, including ourselves, or give us such a sense of guilt and worry that we are constantly trying to prove ourselves and never feeling up to the task.

To follow the Andean path (or any path toward enlightenment) means we need to choose what we want and then give it wings to fly. Doubts and fears fall away when we can trust that we are not alone, dependent only on our human efforts, but are supported and encouraged by a divine resource more powerful than our skills and abilities. This divine power does not judge us by what we produce. It is guided by the force of our intention.

On our way home, we stopped at a lovely restaurant for dinner. I was feeling pretty relaxed, maybe because I didn't have the energy to be stressed out anymore or maybe because I was more at peace with what I had been learning. Simply to be in their physical presence was to be surrounded by a soothing, peaceful, loving energy. During dinner Regis said that he had something he wanted to show me back at the house. He suggested I call Simon to meet us there. It was after 10:00 P.M. when we got home. We sat down at my dining table while Regis unrolled some papers he had in a tube. He laid before us a beautiful drawing of a vision he had received for a universal spirituality center in Peru. It was laid out in the shape of a chakana (Inka cross). In the middle was a circular domed universal temple, surrounded by many other religious buildings in different architectural styles.

As soon as I saw it, I knew I was part of this vision. I knew it was the answer to the question I had asked them when they first arrived: what would I be doing next and where. In a brief moment of deep intuitive knowing, time seemed to stand still. I was at peace and delighted by all aspects of this new opportunity. My first thought was, "Ah yes, it's perfect. Thank you." This tranquil euphoric moment was soon shattered by a panicked need to know my whole job description on the spot, along with the management structure and how it would all be financed.

Regis, Sergio and Simon, caught up in their own excitement, were talking in Spanish without any interest in translating. The more my questions went unanswered, the more frustrated I became. And I was way too tired to be patient. I finally stormed out the room declaring I was going to bed. Used to my histrionics by now, they looked at me and then went back to their discussions.

After a brief rest to calm myself down, I went back out and learned that the vision Regis had was to create a large center where people from all over the world, from all different religions and faith traditions could gather together for spiritual practice and social service. The Sacred Valley near Cusco was an ideal location because of the strong energy vortex there, which would naturally attract people and assist in our efforts for unity and transformation.

That night I committed myself to help him develop the Center even though I wasn't sure what that meant exactly. It all made sense to me on some strange level. Most of my adult life I had created projects before they existed, first as a theatrical producer and later with the outreach ministry. One of my gifts was bringing people together to help make visions a reality, building things from scratch. This was the perfect job for me and a logical next step.

Well, it wasn't really a job in the sense that it had a salary attached to it or an organization to supervise and support my efforts. But I figured since I still had a year left with my current job, some of these other details would fall into place. Intention is everything, I reminded myself. I figured if I was being led to Peru to help develop the Centro Espiritual, then the ways and means would be provided.

The next day I took them to the airport. Several people from the workshop met us there. We sat together until it was time for them to board. I felt incredibly honored to have two such men in my life and they were a good balance for me, with very different personalities and styles of teaching.

Saying good-bye to Regis was especially hard for me. I was beginning to realize that he must be the man I was told about in the jungle—the one I didn't have to look for, the one who would come to me. My connection with Regis, seemed to have an added dimension. Perhaps it was because of the Centro Espiritual and my sense of commitment to that project or the strong connection we had when we met in Urubamba. Perhaps it was because I felt such a deep sense of unconditional love and acceptance from him. It was a feeling that was hard to understand on a logical level that went beyond words or language. So parting was full of sweet sorrow. We promised each other that we would learn to speak the other's language by our next meeting.

I hugged them both and knew we would be seeing each other again. I had already made plans to spend the millennium's New Year in Peru and we had proposals to write about the Centro. It wasn't really good-bye. Still, bringing closure to those incredible, intimate, life-changing days was not easy. Life would never be quite the same, that much I knew. As I drove home alone and entered my now empty house, I wondered what it all meant. Had I really manifested this whole series of events simply by saying, "yes, that's what I want"?

I laughed out loud at the thought because I had been expecting such a different scenario. I thought I was saying yes to a happily ever after romance with my longed-for soulmate. I even went back to read what I'd written in my journal about my experience in the jungle: "There is a man who is very wise and has many things to show you and teach you. He will love you very much. Know if you choose to meet him it will change your life completely. Is that what you want?" "Yes, that's what I want."

Well, there it was, nothing about romance exactly. It was all about seeing my future purpose and calling. And everything She promised me had been delivered, just not in quite the package I was expecting.

So it is with the creative power of "to Want".

Are You Wondering?

I have experienced powerful moments during a weekend workshop or some other event but afterwards, I found it hard to integrate it into my everyday life. How do you do that?

It is often when your guard is down that you have deep powerful experiences because you are open to receiving what your inner wisdom has to show you or teach you. Once you resume the practical aspects of your life, your ego takes over and you begin to doubt the truth of what you experienced. It may seem unbelievable or even absurd. The ego wants to pull you back into what is old and familiar. You must believe there is something more powerful than your skills and abilities, ready to assist you; something bigger, something deeper. Let go of the need for practical proof. Don't make judgments about yourself or your intuition. You can know something deep in your soul without being able to explain it or analyze it. Don't look for outside affirmation. Be clear about your intention and don't get stuck in self-pity or self-criticism because they will only block the access to your inner wisdom.

Try This

When your everyday experiences begin to overshadow the truth of a powerful moment, stay centered and trust you are not alone. The Divine light will guide you if you stay centered in it. Close your eyes. Remember your experience and affirm it. Even say it out loud to yourself. "I believe is the truth."

How do you know the messages you receive are real and valid and not some delusion?

The best way to know that is by practice and experience. Also remember that the message can be valid but your interpretation of the message might be leading you in the wrong direction. Remember my interpretation of the message I received in the jungle about the man I would meet at the conference? I was expecting a "boyfriend" not a teacher, so I was disappointed when my expectation wasn't fulfilled. But somehow I still believed the message I received was a valid one, which of course it turned out to be. When I first saw the plans for the Centro Espiritual, I knew I was part of that project. I knew it was the answer to the question I had been asking for almost a year—where was I going next and what would I be doing? On one level I knew. On other levels I was full of doubts and questions. I wanted someone else to confirm my inner knowing. But with almost every important decision and choice you make, you have to claim it for yourself.

Try This

The next time you receive a message, follow your intuition and see where it leads you. It may turn out to be different than you expected but if it is a message that you resonated strongly with, listen again and ask for clarity. Soon you will be able to determine for yourself when a message rings true and when it is just wishful thinking.

What were the "energy surges" you felt in the tent and why didn't Regis and Sergio explain to you what happened?

I think it was a type of cosmic initiation. Like the karpays which were transmitted by Regis and Sergio during our initiation, this energy transmission that I received while I was sleeping in the tent, was an opening. It was an invitation to claim my calling, not only as a healer but also my role in helping to manifest the vision of the Centro Espiritual in Peru. When a person has a paranormal experience like the one I had, it is hard to explain in material, practical terms, what exactly happened. For this reason, Regis and Sergio honored and affirmed the experience I had without diminishing it with a logical explanation.

TO WANT

Just by wanting something, does that mean you get it? No, but when you are clear what you want and give it your attention, when you visualize it happening, it begins the process of manifesting. It's like you have a bow and arrow. You focus on your target, take aim and then release the arrow. Sometimes it lands on the mark. Sometimes it hits something else. If you are open and conscious, perhaps you are able to recognize that the result, though different from what you originally wanted, might be better. This is the path to Inner Wisdom.

I wanted a job and ended up at seminary, where my life changed in a big way. I wanted a two month cross-cultural experience and ended up doing ministry for nine years with the homeless in South Africa during a rare historical period of socio-political transformation. I ended up with the best "job" I could ever ask for but it certainly wasn't what I had in mind when I was living in New York and looking for employment.

The truth is, even from the beginning, I wanted more than a job. I wanted something meaningful to do with my life that paid me a living wage. And that, I believe, set my intention in motion. Although it took a few years for it to happen, everything along the way was teaching me what I needed to know to accept the opportunity when it came it me.

To want, in the Andean tradition implies a willingness to let the arrow go and see where it lands. It accepts that each of us is part of a larger whole and that different people's intentions are woven together to bring about an elaborate tapestry. Sometimes the things we want simply don't happen. Does this mean we should stop wanting? No.

Ask any inventor or scientist; there are many failed experiments before achieving the desired outcome. And each one teaches you something. If the intention is to manifest, then you must want it and continue to let the arrows of your desire fly.

If you don't know what you want or want nothing, then you become a passive recipient of other people's desires, a pawn on a chess board, blown by the winds of chance. Perhaps your life feels like that sometimes. That is why it is important to name what you want and set your intention clearly. And after that, follow the clues and see where life leads you, what it has to teach you. Become an active player in your own life.

To want, is to say yes to life. Be clear about what you want and set if free to fly. Follow where it leads you and keep setting new intentions at every turn. Be present and aware. You won't be disappointed, at least not for long

SECTION FOUR:
TO KNOW

The Hummingbird and the Condor

In the time before memory, out of the nothingness that was, all that is was created; all the worlds and stars, all the rivers and rocks, every creature and every being.

The people were created without knowing what was beyond them. They did not understand all that was and they longed to see and know what they could not see and know. But the place of the All Knowing was far away in the upper world and the people could not go there.

At this time the condor was the greatest bird. He alone had the strength to fly to the Hanaq Pacha, the upper world, and speak with God. For this reason, all prayers and wishes were sent to the upper world with the great bird. But the condor was not allowed to look on the face of God. No. He would fly as high as he could, then, respectfully, turn his head. When the Divine appeared the condor would deliver the messages without looking, receive the messages for the people, then return to earth. And so it was for as long as there was time.

Now, the hummingbird was the tiniest of birds. She spent her days flying busily from flower to flower drinking in their sweetness. Because she had tasted the nectar of every flower she knew many things. And because of all she knew she had a great desire. She longed to see the face of God. Of course, this was impossible because she was so very small and God so very far away, but her desire grew stronger every day. Then one day out of that strong desire and her great knowledge, an idea grew.

That night, when every creature was asleep she crept up to the condor and nestled deep into his feathers in a place where he could neither see nor feel her. The next morning the condor woke and rose into the sky, higher and higher, until he had reached the Hanaq Pacha. He turned his head, as usual, and God appeared. At that moment, the bold little hummingbird flew out from beneath his feathers and saw God face to face. And, in that same moment, her plumage turned to translucent gold, shining like the rainbow.

Together the hummingbird and the condor returned to earth and since that day they have both been guides to the Upper World; the condor, for his strength and fortitude, and the hummingbird, for her daring and desire to know the face of God.

Chapter 13: The Cosmic Internet

AIR is the element that resides in the North at the top of the chakana, along with the sacred word, To Know. Air is the most basic and primary element of our existence. As we emerge from our mother's wombs we begin life with our first intake of air and we leave this earthly plane when we expel our last breath. And for every minute of every day of every year in between, we are sustained, nurtured, and purified by air. I was told that most human beings only use 10% of the capacity of their lungs to breathe air in and out. 10%. Yet air, through our breath, is one of the best healing regulators that we have at our disposal. If we take three deep breaths in and out, we can relax away anger, tension, fear and other heavy, energy-sapping emotions. Intentional deep breathing can also relieve physical pain in the body.

Air is the primary conductor of communication. When we speak, it is air passing through us that allows our words to have sound; air that allows those words to be delivered and heard by those around us. Microphones, stereo speakers, radios, telephones, televisions all use the airwaves to deliver their sound and image. And in our generation, we have the most amazing technological use of the airwaves to date: the Internet and World Wide Web.

Imagine it—millions of messages and downloaded information flying through the airwaves in split seconds continuously throughout the day, every day, rarely missing their intended destination. There is something innate built into the system that moves messages in the quickest most direct route. If the most probable and direct route is blocked for some reason, the message is immediately transferred to the next most direct route and continues in this fashion until it reaches its desired destination. This happens without anyone working on a message by message basis to decide which is the most direct and open route and how it should be sent there. It just goes there in a split second.

The Internet is not only a wonderfully practical mode of communication but it is an apt metaphor for our own ability to utilize air and energy, not only for communication, but to discover ways of knowing we have only begun to tap. I imagine some internet-like network in the universe—the one that is always conspiring to assist us—that takes our clear intention, our stated desire, and shoots it out toward manifestation in the most probable and direct route. If the intentions of others should block the most direct route then another is found and the desire continues on its path. The more we learn to know and work with this energy, the stronger power we will have to be instruments of transformation in our own lives and the world at large.

The Sacred Word saber (to know) implies this grand concept of knowing. Just imagine if we use only 10% of our lung capacity to breathe, what even smaller percent we use of our ability to know. There are many levels on which we know things. Our current dominant cultures tend to value only the most literal and concrete ways of knowing—things that we can touch, taste, see, and feel. Things that we share a common vocabulary about, things that exist in time and space that can be held and pointed to. These things are called "real". To a slightly lesser extent, our beliefs and concepts are also considered "real" in so far as people can reach general agreement on their definitions. This is probably the reason some religions have spent so much time dogmatizing their beliefs. (i.e., If it is written in a sacred book, then it is true and therefore real.) Currently most of our dominant cultures distrust that which cannot be documented in some concrete, material way.

But more and more, people are beginning to discover other ways of knowing and the vastness of their potential. Take, for instance, the concept of the Internet. Would anyone really believe such a thing were possible if they weren't able to access it from their own desktop PC or the local Internet Café? The vastness of our ability to know and communicate, to send and receive information, to send and receive love and light and healing is beyond our mind's capacity to hold. This is because these other ways of knowing are not centered in our mind/brain, but rather in our heart/soul/spirit. The language is not verbal; it is image and energy. It's an understanding we have when we look at a painting or have a vision during a meditation. Perhaps we can describe it with words but we can't fully capture the experience or the knowledge we derive from the experience because the 'knowing' is not something that happens solely with our mind or our emotions. It is an integrated experience that we have with all levels of our being.

When healers work with image and energy, they can work beyond time and space. The symbol they use becomes the object they wish to transmute. One does not simply represent the other, it becomes the other, mainly through the power of the healers' intention but also because they have learned how to work well with image. Because, on this level, you are not bound by time and space, you can shift things more easily and more permanently than when you work on a physical or literal level.

For example: the night Regis did the public talk after our first level initiation, I was able to speak with the crowd in a way that shifted the energy in the room—and therefore the sensations of each person in the room—without having to spend time talking individually to each person there who was upset because we were not starting on time. Later, during the question and answer session when I was struggling for control, I was back down on the literal/verbal level dealing much less effectively with calming the crowd. Had I been more practiced in consciously using image or more aware that I had the power to do so, I could have handled the end of that night as well as I inadvertently handled the beginning.

Working with energy is even harder to comprehend with our logical thinking minds than working with image, because energy is everything and everywhere. It is a luminous thread that connects creation and all of us to each other and to the infinite. For this reason, it can be used to transmute, transform and heal anything, anywhere. It is where intentions and desires are born. In the world of science, it is a fact that energy organizes matter and therefore creates the physical. I don't have much of a mind for science but I do know that the reason Regis can see and know things about people he has never met or heal people from a distance is that he has mastered the art of working with energy and connecting with the Divine.

The principles of quantum physics and chaos theory, of which I know very little, explain "The Butterfly Effect"; how a butterfly flapping its wings in Africa can affect a storm that will happen in California. When we learn to work with energy, beyond the frameworks of time and space, we can stop the storm before it starts, working with the butterfly. Once the storm has hit California, it is much more difficult to deal with its effects. This is a metaphor for why it is important to learn to work with image and energy. On these levels we can have greater impact with less effort in the work of healing and transformation of our inner beings and with others.

When Regis and Sergio first taught us to work with the four elements and nature, it seemed strange to me. Lying on the ground, hugging a tree, or meditating with my feet in the water, I felt a bit self-conscious. However, the more I developed my relationship with the four elements and the forces of nature, the more I began to know and experience things on deeper levels. I began to know what the elements know. The elements and nature communicate through image and energy and I was able to learn from them. We of course, are part of nature and have the capacity for this innate knowing but it is a language and ability that most of us haven't learned or practiced. This is the kind of "knowing" to which the Sacred Word saber refers.

Air is energy and moves freely through time and space. When we know Air, converse with it, travel with it, move freely on its wings, then we can also tap into its deep wisdom and knowledge of the ages. It broadens our perspective.

Imagine yourself in a closet or a small room of your house. Imagine if the world was only what you could see and touch. Now imagine that you could lift the roof off your house and hover above it. Not only could you see all the rooms of your house but also the neighborhood it is in and other people around it. As you move farther up you can see the whole city, the region. We can spend a lot of time rearranging the furniture in our house or we can expend the same effort shifting the energy in such a way that we improve the condition of the whole region, which includes our house but is not limited to it.

For example, Nelson Mandela was a political prisoner in South Africa for 27 years, where he lived in a small dingy cell with few material objects. He could have narrowed his perspective to the confines of that cell and become an embittered man. But he made other choices. He expanded his perceptions to imagine the impossible. He refused to be bound by the limits his captors placed on him. Eventually, he was able to convince them that it was better for everyone to negotiate a form of power sharing that acknowledged the humanity of the oppressed majority. He had to transform the thinking of not only his captors but also his own people who were sure he had become a traitor to their cause. Did his efforts get him out of prison? Yes, but he was more interested in everyone getting out of the prison-like system that was destroying South Africa, than simply working to get himself released.

Did Nelson Mandela (and others who assisted in that miraculous transition) learn to work with image and energy in the way I am describing here? I don't know. But I do know that something beyond the force of people's material efforts, beyond the force of economic sanctions, beyond the brutal guerrilla warfare that raged for years, shifted the feelings and beliefs of the majority of South Africans, including the ones holding political power and the ones dedicated to military overthrow. This quantum shift transformed not only the government and political system in South Africa, but more importantly it forever changed the way people of all races acknowledge one another's humanity there.

The more of us that learn this art, this language, this knowledge, the more possible it will be to bring about the tariypay pachca, the golden age of harmony and well being that the Inka prophecies tell us is just within our grasp. When I first heard that there were healers in Peru that possessed this knowledge, I wanted more than anything to learn it too.

Are You Wondering?

How do I learn to work with this energy?
Practice, practice, practice.

Try This

Start by becoming more conscious of your breathing. Breath more deeply and more slowly. Feel your breath filling all the areas of your body, not just your lungs. Imagine this energy entering your system and purifying all your organs and expanding your consciousness. If you have a place you can go outside on a hilltop or a mountain, sit and meditate there. Feel the breeze on your face and your skin. Call the wind and see if it comes to you. Engage in conversation with the wind, with the air. Give thanks for its life giving breath, its refreshing breeze. Imagine that you are part of this vast cosmic internet and ask for assistance with your ability to communicate with it and through it. Ask, "Expand my consciousness. Amplify my awareness. Elevate my vibration so I may see and know as you see and know."

What do you mean when you say we only use a small percent of our ability to know?
They say your senses take in 20 times more bites of information than your brain can process at any given moment. Perhaps you have played the game where you are shown a picture and then asked questions about what you saw or remember seeing after the picture is removed from your sight. Usually people noticed or remembered only a few items.

You can train yourself to see beyond what you expect to see or have grown accustomed to seeing. There is a vast universe out there of which you have experienced very little. Humans tend to see (experience with all our senses) only that with which we are familiar or have grown accustom. So in order to see and know more, you must push yourself into the new and unfamiliar. By working with the elements of nature, you increase the awareness of your senses— your five physical senses (sight, touch, taste, smell and hearing), as well as your sixth sense (perception). These practices will open your awareness in the routine of your everyday life. You will learn to see beyond the familiar. Your consciousness will expand to take in more and greater possibilities. Your ability to know will grow.

Try This
* Feel the water of the river flowing through your toes as you sit on the shore and perceive your heavy energy being washed away.
* Smell the sweet fragrance of a flower and touch its soft delicate petals. Listen for what it has to teach you.
* Lie on the ground and talk with mother earth. Give her your frustration and anxiety to use as fertilizer to enrich her soil. Perceive her gratitude. Put your ear to the ground and hear her guidance.
* Stare into the flame of a burning candle or a blazing fire. Feel the heat, note the smell, and perceive the energy within the flame. Engage with it.

Chapter 14: Beginning to Know

After Regis and Sergio came to Johannesburg for our Inka workshop I was on fire with all the things I had been taught, the things I knew. Life would be different now! I had no idea how different it would really be.

In March the interim leadership at the church who took over after Vernon's resignation, made some policy changes in our housing project without consulting those of us most directly involved. Their attitude in general to the outreach ministry was very different than we were used to under Vernon's leadership.

It was unbearable seeing the project that I had worked so hard to shape dismantled before my eyes. At first, I reasoned with them, but they didn't seem to hear me. So then I fell back into old patterns of pushing and fighting to "save" a ministry that had been the focus of my life for eight years. I was frustrated, angry, and eventually exhausted. If they thought they could do the job better than me without any experience or insight into the community—fine! They could have it.

In that exhausted release, I recognized an opportunity to disengage, both emotionally and practically. Once I was able to see the behavior of the new leadership was actually the universe conspiring to assist me (rather than totally frustrate me), I was able to let go of some of my "work" responsibilities and focused more on my new life that was unfolding

My intuitive response to the vision of the Centro Espiritual had become, in my mind, a plan. When my commitments to Global Ministry were complete, I would move to Peru. I would help Regis develop the spirituality center.

Even that was frustrating.

Regis was slow in responding to my email queries for details on how to proceed. I wanted to write a proposal, but didn't know his intended audience. I wanted a clearer idea of my job description. But obviously Andean shamans didn't work on the same business model as me. Once again, I had to let it go.

It was all so confusing. Why were there times in my life, like going to seminary or South Africa, when my intuition led me down a path where doors flung open and I simply walked through? My insights about the Centro Espiritual and Peru had been no less clear or powerful. Why wasn't this easy?

At the same time there were incredible dreams, insights, and inspirations reminding me that I was on the path to a new life, even if I didn't have all the details. I remember one healing workshop where the energy just flowed out of me. Even the announcements were inspirational. One Sunday healing service I felt a tugging on my liturgical robe and looked around, seeing no one. But I knew there was a Presence with me. That night I felt it strongly, but it was always there when I needed it even in my dreariest moments.

As the year progressed, I became more conscious about the way I was living, no longer comfortable reacting to situations the old way, and yet I had not completely fashioned a new way either. I had a dream in which I was studying law in some outdoor, earth-colored setting. I was being given lots of information, but I really didn't understand it. It was just words. There was a man in the dream with me, a friend. We were walking together after the class and I saw light patterns in the sky. There was a huge bird above us, a condor or eagle, which stayed close to us throughout the rest of the dream. I told him that this was a very good sign, but in truth I didn't know what exactly it meant. Throughout the dream I was naive or dense, I just wasn't getting the significance of what I was being given. My psyche was speaking to me about integrating what I had been learning, about knowing information on a different level than understanding simply what words mean. I was moving on trust now, on knowing what I did not know, that somehow all would be well and I would be led to exactly the right thing.

I felt a stronger need to be outside with the elements, so for my weekend off in May I went to a beautiful small retreat center built on a mountain near where we did our first level initiation. It was run by a Catholic priest who also did Zen Buddhist meditation and yoga (having spent seven years in India). Most of the weekend I was silent surrounded by the beauty of nature and the view of the lake below. I felt clearer about my plans to move to Peru. The Interfaith aspect of this retreat center reminded me of the Centro Espiritual and felt like a confirmation that I was indeed moving in the right direction.

The next week, I lead a healing workshop at the church that turned out to be very powerful. I later told my Spiritual Director, Michelle that I had been facilitating a healing workshop once a week for more than two years, trusting that healing was taking place. But that day I knew I was a healer. I felt such a relaxed comfortable sense of myself, strong and clear and calm. There was no doubt in me and also no sense of self-importance. I simply was present and allowed the healing to flow through me. Because I had a strong sense of knowing, the power to communicate and confer healing was also stronger than before. The profound simplicity of it felt solid and real.

Clearly new levels of knowing were awakening in me even though I wasn't always sure how to interpret and use them. Slowly, I was learning to be present, trusting that everything I needed would come to me as I needed it. In the old days, I had spent a great deal of time and effort seeking to control the outcome of things. I would have a flash of inspiration and clarity, then start to work as hard as I could to manifest my version of how things were to be, how I would arrive at that destination. I wanted to get on the express train and take no detours until I reached my goal. Now that yearning I had carried with me since I was three (and felt more intensely than ever) appeared to be something more than finding a soul mate or the perfect job. The longing was not for a person found or an outcome accomplished but an expanded consciousness, peacefulness, and a sense of oneness with all that is. There was no destination, no train to get on or off, only a place of vast possibilities and opportunities to become my best self.

What I know now is that inspiration, insight, and intuition exist on a different level of consciousness. In that place, not only is the vision easier to have, it is also easier to manifest. And you do that, not by reaching for your rolodex and day planner projecting into the future, but by being completely present and open every moment. When we reach back down to that mundane level where timelines exist, we cut ourselves off from the extraordinary flow of the other level of knowing. It is challenging to live this way because not only do we need to learn a new way of being, we have to unlearn the old way of doing.

Now, as most of my life was up in the air, I was discovering how much easier and more effective it was to use the power of my intention (image and energy) rather than the force of my will (physical and mental).

During one of my daily meditations in June, I received a "message" to invite Regis and Sergio to come back to South Africa in December to do another workshop with us. It was one of those things that made no logical sense. Planning another workshop weeks before completing my job and my life in Johannesburg, seemed a bit foolish. Plus it was unlikely that Regis and Sergio would be able to return that soon. But, I had learned to respect the messages that came to me in my meditations and decided I would write them about the idea. A few weeks later, they both agreed to come for another workshop in December and said they would do the second level initiation for any of the paqos who were interested.

"Oh well," I thought, "at least this time I know what I'm planning and I have enough advance notice to advertise a bit more." I was actually quite pleased and trusted that their visit and the next level initiation would help me bring closure to my life in South Africa, rather than create more anxiety.

In August, I agreed to be on an interfaith panel for the Johannesburg Press launch of the World Parliament of Religions that would be held in Cape Town that December. I think they wanted a woman on the panel, which they weren't going to find among the Rabbis, Catholic priests, Imams, and Buddhist monks. So there I was, down at City Hall in a room full of 100 or so reporters and spectators.

The organizer who requested my participation, assured me that the launch would be informal and that I didn't need to prepare a speech. But once I was seated on the stage behind the bank of microphones next to all those religious men, I was feeling a bit unprepared. Each of us was asked say a few words about our respective religions and why we supported the World Parliament of Religions. The Rabbi and the Imam both read prepared speeches that were uninspiring and had little to do with interfaith dialogue.

The atmosphere in the room was restless. I wondered what I was going to say but reminded myself to breathe and be present and trust that the words would come to me. As I stood up, I took a moment to make eye contact with the people and said, "Hi, I'm Diane…" Then the words just flowed out of me. While I was speaking, something interesting was happening to the energy in the room. One part of me kept talking with the words coming from some source that wasn't my thinking brain. Another part of me was observing how engaged people were becoming, as if they had woken up from a nap. I felt the heavy energy that had previously filled the room dissipating and being replaced by a lightness that brought smiles to people's faces. I was aware of myself as the speaker, deeply engaged and present with the audience. But I was also aware of an energetic power that was flowing through me and throughout the room. It felt magical.

When I sat down, I knew something very powerful had just happened but I couldn't quite believe that I was the vehicle through which it was orchestrated. The whole tone of the proceedings changed after I spoke. The next speaker put aside his written speech and spoke from his heart instead, as did the remaining two.

After the formalities ended, many people came up to speak to me, saying how moved they were by what I had said. Thinking of the Centro Espiritual, I was encouraged to see how people from different backgrounds and religions could share so excitedly with one another. It was as if a door had been opened and many people were choosing to walk through it.

I realized it wasn't so much what I said that shifted the attention of the audience, but rather that I had been so open, which allowed the message to come from a very deep loving place. And love is a powerful energy. It was similar to the night I spoke before Regis' talk about Inka Spirituality. In both cases, I had a strong feeling of love and compassion for the people I was addressing.

I was beginning to learn that this other-worldly sensation only happened when I was totally present in the situation, centered in myself, without having any desire to prove what I was saying or elicit a certain outcome from the people I was addressing. My intention was simply to speak from my heart, connecting with love and positive energy. I also intentionally called on the power of the spirit to speak through me. The difference between what happened at the Press Launch and other times, was that I was able to sense it consciously while it was happening, to observe it and still be present, watching it flow through me without my ego getting in the way.

I was learning how to be present and recognizing that we can only truly know things in the present moment. Living in the present, life feels open and uncluttered. The need to push or fret or fight is diminished. I had spent a great deal of energy in my life fretting about the past or pushing to make things happen in a certain way. I'd feel frustrated or hurt when things didn't go the way I wanted. Now I was discovering how much easier and more fulfilling life was by being conscious of the benevolent universal force that was teaching me new ways of knowing.

Are You Wondering?

How do you learn to be present?

Learning to be present starts by being aware of your thoughts and your conversations. Observe when you are thinking or talking about things that have already happened. Notice when your attention is focused on what might happen in the future. How does it make you feel? Anxious? Sad? Happy? Frustrated? Whenever your thoughts and words are someplace other than here and now, you are missing what is happening in the present or at best, you are only remotely conscious of them. It is only in the present that you can accomplish something. The past is gone and the future is yet to unfold. The more present you are, the more able you are to expand your awareness. The more conscious you become in "the now", the deeper perceptions you will develop. As you amplify your perceptions and awareness, you increase your ability to know, to understand, to navigate the ambiguities of life. By being in the present you can better hear the voice of your inner wisdom.

Try This

Learn to be in the present by observing when you are not. For 30 minutes carefully observe your behavior and keep bringing your focus back to the present. When you hear yourself telling your friend a story about something that happened to you in the past, stop for a moment and look her/him in the eye. Observe his mood. Smile and ask her how she is doing. Share with him what you observe. Notice how it makes you feel to be present and open with your friend. Notice if you have difficulty looking her in the eye. Be aware of your surroundings. Are there birds chirping outside? Are there other people in the room? What color shirt is your friend wearing? Each time you observe that your thoughts or words are about the past or the future, bring yourself back into the present. Do this at least once a week. Soon it will become easier and your awareness of life around you will grow.

You spoke of two levels of knowing: Physical/Mental and Image/Energy. Can you explain the difference?

Physical/mental knowing is the kind with which you are most familiar. It is knowing how to read and write and count. It is the kind of knowing you learn in school and that you use in the everyday activities of your life.

Knowing with image and energy is processed through your intuition and perception. It is the knowing you experience during meditation or through energy healing. It is when you know something has happened but you cannot explain it logically.

Try This

Go to a public place like a cafe or a park. Sit down and close your eyes. Wait for someone to sit down near you. Sense who the person is. Use your intuition. Feel the energy around that person. What can you tell about them, without hearing them speak or seeing what they look like?

Chapter 15: The Nature of Things

In mid-September, during one of our weekly healing work-shops at the church, I was leading an inner child meditation. I saw DiDi on the swing in Cincinnati when I was three, so joyful and connected with nature and God. I also saw her at a similar age feeling alone and isolated because she had done something "wrong" or "bad" and was being punished. I realized that I car-ried an old fear of being rejected and alone. Then my higher self reminded me that I was also "alone" on the swing but still con-nected with everything. In the meditation I felt assurance that I am "good" and whole and always was.

The next night I had a dream in which there was a major dis-pute going on that I was trying to mediate. My higher self in the dream realized that the only hope for change in the world was to rise above logic and fairness and allow universal love to take over; that we needed to let go of the injury, no matter how terrible. In the dream, as well as my semi-lucid state, I knew it was very significant.

The next day I discussed it with my Spiritual Director Michelle. I told her that since I was young I had resisted the notion that life was limited or small. I kept resisting the restric-tions that were put on me (which didn't go over big with the nuns at my Catholic schools). I was often told I was bad or wrong. But now I realized it wasn't true. I was being true to what I knew about God and life. Now those wounds were being healed and I was moving to a 'higher' level. This was reflected in the dream where I no longer felt the need to make the person wrong or hate them for what they did but rather to recognize 'the way it is' and let it go with love.

I was beginning to really understand that as I became more unconditionally loving of myself, then I could also be that way with others, without having to make them "wrong" because I knew that I wasn't wrong either. I was learning to appreciate what IS rather than be upset by what ISN'T. It made life so much easier and allowed me to recognize the gift in everything that was unfolding. There is so much love and joy to be had if we open ourselves to it. And more and more I was feeling it.

The outreach ministry at the church was slowing down. We told the community we were closing at the end of the year and we had meetings at which people could process their feelings about it. I kept my distance from the interim leadership, releasing my frustrations and concerns with how they were handling things. This meant I had more time to focus on my own processing, which I increasingly saw as a much-appreciated gift. My focus shifted from doing to being.

Sharing with the community about what the outreach ministry had meant to them was very touching. It helped me realize the biggest gift of the ministry for me was learning to see and experience beauty in the midst of ugliness, and joy in the midst of poverty and pain. I had heard such wisdom from the people I worked with, most of whom had little formal education, who were unvalued by society. And more than anything so many of us had experienced love in the midst of loneliness. Because of that I know that one can experience beauty, joy and love anywhere, anytime, under any circumstance. It was a very big gift I was taking with me into my new life in Peru.

Not to say that everything in those last few months of my life in South Africa was smooth and easy. The prospect of selling all my things (house, car, furniture, etc.) to move to an undefined future without formal employment in a country whose language I didn't yet speak was cause for occasional anxiety.

In my meditation one mid-October morning, I found myself thinking about all my household stuff and could feel my anxiety rising. Then I heard a voice saying, "let go and rise above". I got on the back of an eagle and flew up into the sky. I could see my house far below and small. Then I saw Peru and the Centro Espiritual and thousands of lives transforming. I heard the assurance of the magnificence awaiting me. It helped me let go and trust in the beauty of all that was and was becoming; to stay focused on what really matters and let go of the rest.

Two weeks before Regis and Sergio arrived for the second Inka Spirituality workshop, I went down to Cape Town for a long weekend to visit a very close friend. She did a guided meditation with me where she asked me to invite my soul being from the future into my body. The feeling was one of great solidarity, assurance and strength. I had the sense that the Centro Espiritual would not be directly occupying me for a while; that it would take about ten years to really be operating. But there was no cause for anxiety because I would be doing many other things. I saw myself traveling quite a bit. The strongest message I received was to trust and know that everything would go smoothly, that new things were ready to fill the space created by all I was releasing.

The preparations for the workshop had gone remarkably smoothly. Over forty people had registered, which covered all my expenses. The day before Regis and Sergio arrived I met with Michelle and described how calm I'd been about things. "I could have put myself into a spin regarding a number of issues but because I didn't, I ended up having more time than I needed to get everything done." I realized that being fully in the present one creates the feeling of having 'more time' because of what usually gets spent on projecting the future or worrying about the past.

When I met Regis and Sergio at the airport the next day, it was as if no time had passed since our farewell eleven months before. We spoke about the workshop and second-level initiation, as well as plans for the Centro Espiritual and my upcoming trip to Peru. The workshop was being held at a larger venue this time so we drove out there for them to see it and scout the right locations for our work with the elements.

It poured rain all night and the next day. But just before the opening afternoon session, as if on cue, the rain stopped. I watched Regis and Sergio interacting with the anxious participants and smiled as I remembered how I had been the first time, wanting to know and understand everything before experiencing it for myself. I felt so much more able to be present and open.

They spoke about the chakana and the priestly levels in the Andean tradition. They also seemed more relaxed than the first time. It was wonderful to hear it all again.

Before dinner we did a despacho for Pachamama (Earth), which was lovely and powerful. During the ritual offering I felt filled with love and gratitude for their presence and for all I was learning and becoming. We were each given a coca leaf into which we put our intention or request. I asked that during the second level initiation, that I would be able to "see" with my third eye.

After dinner we had a big fire with fifty of us forming a circle around it. Each person shared in turn, how they were feeling. This group seemed more relaxed and open than at the first workshop. Or perhaps it was just that I was more relaxed.

The second day began with a session about the element Water followed by a despacho. During the meditation I was overcome by a bittersweet joy for my life and work in South Africa and how it had prepared me for all that was unfolding. Toward the end of the despacho, I noticed a young woman named Paula who seemed to be struggling with some internal issues. I sensed her fragility and began sending her love, imaging a golden light around her. Shortly after that Regis went over to her and began working with her. I was so touched to see the abundance of his unconditional love surrounding her. I was also delighted by the synchronicity of both of us noticing Paula's distress at the same time.

Just as I was beginning to think that nothing could ever disrupt the state of bliss I was floating in, Sergio made some offhanded comment to me at lunch. It triggered my old pattern of feeling rejected because I wasn't performing up to standard. Even my stomach began to feel upset. So much for unabated bliss.

I was determined not to 'get stuck' in my emotions and fortunately that afternoon we did practical exercises with Earth and Water at a nearby park with a beautiful river running through it. We started with each person selecting a tree to embrace, connecting with the energy of the tree and listening to what it had to tell us. I had a very difficult time getting centered let alone connecting with the tree. Ants were crawling all over my feet and sandals, mirroring the clawing thoughts that I couldn't seem to let go of. I changed trees three or four times and still couldn't get settled. Finally I sat down on the ground with my back to a tree that was closer to the center of the group. I felt better.

The next exercise was with Mother Earth. We each lay down with our bellies on the ground, to converse with our loving mother. We were invited to give her all our heavy energy, our anxieties and frustrations (our 'shit') that she lovingly receives as fertilizer to enrich her soil. In this exchange, is life-giving reciprocity. I gladly gave her all my angst and heard back an affirming reassurance that everything would unfold just as it should—the closure of my life in South Africa and the beginning of my new life in Peru. She even told me that Sergio had only the best intentions for me and my growth, and I was able to hear and believe it was so.

By the time we finished the two water meditations, (further releasing whatever remained of our hurts and fears), I felt balanced again—clear, clean and at peace. I marveled again at the grand simplicity of our work with the elements. How could something so easy and so readily available be so miraculous! To do these practices not only clears us of our anxieties but also enables us to develop a deeper relationship with the elements so we can know what they know. They become our teachers, feeding and healing us as we learn. All without condition or price, because the exchange is reciprocal. This is the way of nature, the way of God's creation.

In all of the exercises though, there was part of me that felt I wasn't connecting, that my mind was chattering. Yet by the time I finished I could feel the results of the connections my deeper self was making and the 'chatter' was part of releasing deeply stored emotions.

The fire that night after dinner was the most exquisite spectacle of dancing flames I had ever seen. Sparks of light rose up from the embers flying into the dark starry sky. We could feel the energy and delight of the spirits. Each person spoke about their experiences with the elements. The love and appreciation was palpable and seemed to fuel the fire as it danced with delight. After everyone shared, Regis and Sergio taught us how to eat stars. Sergio's eyes sparkled with Puckish delight as he warned us not to eat too many because the energy from them would keep us awake and tomorrow was another day.

Day three was about the element Air. During the despacho, South Africa's equivalent to a hummingbird had flown into the conference room and hovered over Regis as he knelt before the ritual offering on the floor. It was as if she was watching with approval and appreciation. After a few minutes the bird flew to the highest part of the thatched roof, hovering above the despacho and then flew away. In the Andean tradition, the hummingbird, along with the condor, is the guardian of the North, where the element of Air resides.

That afternoon after lunch we climbed the mountain on the conference center's property. The day was clear, hot and sunny. The climb was a bit strenuous but the view from the top was a spectacular reward. We filled our lungs with life-giving air, the further and higher we climbed. Once we all assembled on top to begin our first exercise/meditation, an eagle appeared in the sky, soaring above and around us. (The eagle is the spiritual counterpart to the condor, the other guardian of the North.)

Then we closed our eyes as Regis and Sergio summoned the wind. A gentle breeze began to blow and I could feel myself flying with the eagle and floating on the currents of air, free and expansive. The wind ebbed and flowed throughout the meditation. At one point I felt Regis approach me from behind. The breeze was soft and gentle on my face. Regis then blew with force on the back of my neck and suddenly a gust of wind hit me with such velocity from the front that I lost my balance. These moments of mystical synchronicity no longer surprised me but continued to delight and amaze me. Who were these men that possessed the power to play so majestically with the forces of nature? Was it possible for me to know how to do such things? This was indeed my intention.

The last day of the workshop began early. We were all to meet at 5:00 A.M. for a special sunrise ceremony. I was awakened at 3:30 A.M. by thunder and lightening and a deluge of rain. I lay in bed for a while wondering what we were going to do. At 4:30 I went to consult with Regis and Sergio. They seemed reasonably calm and said we would continue with our plans. It was still pouring rain as we prepared to leave our building and meet the others on the central lawn. As soon as we stepped outside the rain slowed and then stopped.

We walked in procession to an east-facing vista on the side of the mountain. The clouds filled the horizon even as I could feel Regis and Sergio willing them to part. The rays of the morning sun broke through the cracks in the clouds as the music played and the incense burned. It wasn't as spectacular as the sunrise we had during the first workshop but it beautiful in other ways.

After breakfast, they spoke about Fire and we made our last despacho of the workshop. By lunchtime, the sky was clear and blue, the day hot and sunny. We had a two-hour break and most of us played in the pool like happy children from a big loving family. Paula seemed to glow with a new vitality and everyone seemed light and happy. It was as if we had all fallen in love with each other or fallen in love with life.

We assembled on the lawn about 3:00 P.M. to learn how to create wind. We ran around flapping our arms up and down in a specific way that Sergio showed us. We could feel the breeze it made under our arms but we laughed at ourselves running around not sure if we were being teased or whether this was a 'serious' exercise in learning to control the elements. But soon our laughter turned into an incredulous silent awe as a mighty wind began to blow and thunder crackled in the distance.

Before we had much time to think about what happened, it was time to light the fire that would burn the despachos we had prepared the previous days and that morning. As we formed a large circle around the fire, Regis and Sergio shook their Andean rattles and chanted. The fire was lit and the despachos placed on top of the quadrangle layers of logs, which stood about four feet high.

The storm we had summoned with our wind exercise was drawing closer and closer. Flashes of lightening lit the darkening sky and the raindrops seemed to pause mid-air as Regis and Sergio willed them to wait just a little longer as the flames crawled higher to ignite our sacred offerings. We held hands as we watched the fire in meditative silence, sure that the rain would burst forth at any moment. A clap of thunder broke the silence and then an electrical charge flew around the circle through our hands.

I looked around to see if others had felt what I felt. Lightening had struck just as the flames began to consume our despachos. The wide-eyed grins on people's faces, spoke the truth of what had just happened. We stood still not wanting to let go of each other's hands, but we had been told that only the highest-level shamans are permitted to watch the actual burning of the despachos, because the energy is said to be very strong. It was time for us to go.

As we turned away and began to walk back to the conference room, the skies opened and the downpour with which the predawn morning began, returned to bring closure on the day and the weekend. It was quite a stunning display, with all the elements participating. Back in the conference room, each person had a chance to share what the weekend had meant to them. I remembered the last time, eleven months before, and marveled at the transformation that had occurred within me. Once again I was deeply touched by other people's experiences, the love and appreciation we all felt for Regis and Sergio, and the awesome beauty of the healing and awakening they brought to us.

I didn't have much time however, to bask in the glow of that love and gratitude. Twenty-five people had signed up to do the first level initiation that would be happening the next day. Eleven of us would be doing the second level initiation the two days after that. Then Sergio would do a two-day Rieki workshop, assisted by Regis. All this required organization, in the midst of saying good-byes and clearing out the auditorium so the next group could come in.

I should have known by now that resting on one's laurels was not part of the program when Regis and Sergio were around. Still, I can't say I was prepared for what it was they expected of me next.

Are You Wondering?

You mentioned a dream where you understood the importance of letting go of an injury, no matter how grave. How is that possible?

In my dream I had a profound understanding of the importance of forgiveness, and acceptance. The truth of this understanding is something I still hold dearly. When you can forgive an injury that someone has done, you are able to recognize your own humanity as well as the humanity of the other. It sets you both free to accept each other and yourself, to recognize that you both are human beings who make mistakes. Forgiveness allows for healing and transformation to occur. It melts the barriers that divide and isolate you from others and from the divine. If you are angry or bitter or frustrated, your awareness of the other and of the divine is blocked from reach. You become diminished. You become closed. Your life force drains away.

When you can forgive and accept that the circumstances are as they are, it frees you to become your best self. In the moment of forgiveness you are flooded with grace and many more possibilities exist than when you hold hate in your heart. Forgiveness defies logic. It doesn't make sense that you should let go of some horrible evil thing that someone has done. Your logical mind tells you it is wrong. Evil must be punished. But the truth is punishment does not resolve evil, it only perpetuates it. The golden rule is golden because it brings about peace—do unto others, as you want others to do unto you. Sometimes you think that your actions are unforgivable, so you judge others in the same way. Forgiveness frees both the forgiver and the forgiven.

The Truth and Reconciliation Commission was established in South Africa after Nelson Mandela became president. It was one of the most powerful healing acts the new government set in motion. They decided not to punish people who had committed political crimes during the apartheid years. If people came forward and told the truth about their atrocities, they would be given immunity. Victims could testify as well as perpetrators. I witnessed the mother of a slain black youth testify. The man responsible for killing her young son also testified how they beat the boy and threw the body in a shallow grave. He explained where the body was buried. He wept and asked the mother's forgiveness. She embraced him, also in tears and thanked him for telling her the truth. This is one of many moving stories of unbelievable acts of forgiveness and healing. The testimonies of this commission helped to heal the soul of a nation, which is now prospering after many years of violence and struggle.

I believe that forgiveness and acceptance are truly our only hope for real healing and transformation. It requires of us a broad vision—letting go of our limited notions of right and wrong, good and evil. It requires instead a deep compassionate understanding of the nature of human beings. Love alone heals. Through forgiveness and acceptance our capacity to love and be loved expands.

Try This

Think of something you have done in your life for which you have difficulty forgiving yourself. Close you eyes. Imagine that black South African mother embracing you and saying that she forgives you. Imagine that she is offering you divine love and unconditional acceptance. Allow yourself to feel that love wash over you.

Now think of someone you have had difficulty forgiving. Close your eyes and see that person. Imagine yourself hugging that person and saying, "I forgive you". Feel the divine love washing over both of you, held in that embrace. Give thanks to God that such a thing is possible. If you have trouble doing this exercise, repeat it daily until you feel the love flowing freely.

Chapter 16: Another Way of Knowing

It was dark by the time we started driving back to my house. I had given all the new first level initiates their instructions and arranged for one of them to pick up Regis and Sergio in the morning because I had to work at the church. I breathed a sigh of relief that my duties were completed. As a magnanimous gesture, I said I'd drive up to get them at the end of the day if they would like. After all, it was only 90 minutes drive from my house.

Then Regis and Sergio started to list all the things they needed me to get for the initiation. Each person would be given a mesa, a medicine bundle wrapped in Peruvian material Regis and Sergio had brought from Cusco, but each 'manta' had to be cut and the edges sewn. We needed twenty-five shells and twenty-five malachite eggs that would be placed inside each mesa, along with other elements. I didn't own a sewing machine nor did I have the faintest idea where to get twenty-five shells. I knew where to buy malachite eggs but it was nowhere near my house, plus I had to work in the morning. I was stunned that they had waited until this late hour to organize these things. "How can I do that?"

Sergio responded, "You want to reach higher levels but you don't want to work?"

Before my ego had a chance to be hurt, I remembered that during the despacho that morning, the intention I had placed into my coca leaf was to move on this path to the highest level that I was able. I wanted to learn all there was to know and nothing mattered to me more. A strange calmness came over me and I realized that I would be able to do whatever it was that they asked of me. "OK." I said.

After that, my relationship with them shifted. We worked from 8:30 P.M. until after midnight organizing things for the next day. I called Theresa who was letting us use her farm again for both the first and second level initiations. She had the shells. Sue, who was picking up Regis and Sergio in the morning, lived near a place that sold malachite eggs and said she would be happy to get them for me. I counted the money that had to be banked in the morning, trusting I would find someone to sew the mantas. As each task was completed they would remember something else they needed. Reiki manuals needed to be copied and bound. Ok, there was a copy place next door to the bank, where I would stop on the way to work.

A problem that would have seemed impossible to me only days before, was solved before I had time to question that it might not be. Talk about the universe conspiring to assist! I felt like I had been transported to some magical kingdom where you just had to wish to make it so. Could one take up permanent residency here, I wondered.

Then, after all the first level plans were complete, they said, "We need a sick person for the second level initiation on Thursday." "A sick person?" "Yes, we want you to perform a healing, to demonstrate to the group. Part of the purpose of the second level is to awaken one's healing powers. You have healing power already but the initiation will increase your ability." I looked at them for a silent moment, from my spot in the magical kingdom and thought, "If they think I can do this then I presume I will be able to do it." So I answered, "Alright, I'll call Theresa and ask her if she knows someone who lives near her farm."

And of course she did, and that too was set in place. The healing… well, that was still more than two days away. I had plenty to deal with before then. I finally went to bed and slept like a baby until 5:30 A.M. After the guys left an hour later, I even had time to do a relaxing meditation. I wrote in my journal "I feel a deep awakening within me and more clarity than ever that the knowledge and vision I seek is within me, springing to life."

On my way to work I found a sidewalk vendor with a sewing machine who said he could hem the material and have all the mantas ready by noon. I dropped off the Rieki manual to be copied and bound and arrived at the church right on time. I lead a very powerful healing workshop, where all the participants left with smiles on their faces and a bounce in their walk—including me. I then left to go to the bank, pick up the manuals and the mantas and was on the road. About an hour into the drive, I began marveling that I had actually pulled it off and would arrive with time to spare. I felt invincible. And with that small rise of my ego-self, I was tipped off balance. Imperceptively at first, but then quite obviously.

I parked the car at the bottom of the mountain and opened the trunk to take out all the things I had brought, including my own ceremonial poncho that Regis had given me during the previous workshop. I could feel myself rushing a bit for I could see the group far at the top. I put as much as I could in my backpack and had the other things in a bag. Then the zipper broke on my backpack. For ten frustrating minutes I struggled to close it with the sun blazing down on me and mosquitoes nipping at my exposed skin. I prayed, I breathed, I tried to calm myself but I had fallen back down to earth and couldn't get back to my mystical place. Finally, I decided to leave the poncho and backpack, climbing the mountain with only the mantas and other items for the mesas.

Regis had seen me from above and must have sensed my distress. He walked part way down the hill with one of the other participants to meet me and help carry the supplies. The initiates were in meditative silence, so there was no chance to explain what happened. Sergio whispered with irritation, "We've been waiting for you." I sat quietly with the rest of the group, trying to release my stress and own irritation. It would take quite a few hours—and some torturous discussions with Regis and Sergio ("What happened to you?") —before my balance returned.

It's only now that I understand more deeply what actually happened. When we are living in that other dimension, where all seems in perfect synchronicity, the vibration is very fine and can be easily tipped off balance if we re-enter the material dimension even for a brief moment. By comparison, our ego-selves have a heavy hand, like an elephant in the china shop. Driving in the car to the mountain, I began looking at what had been happening since the night before, marveling at my power to perform the impossible. But once I was outside looking in, I was no longer present in the 'magical kingdom'. And I lost the power.

Have you ever seen one of those posters that has a geometric pattern but if you look at it long enough and loosen your focus sufficiently, you can see a three-dimensional picture inside? Once you see the picture inside the pattern, you wonder how you could have missed it because it is so vivid and obvious. Yet if you blink or become distracted even for a moment, it disappears and all that remains is the opaque geometric design. That's something like the delicacy of our ability to access that other way of knowing, of being. Once you are in it, you can stay in it, seeing the interior picture as clear as can be, where magic is the lingua franca. But if we break the flow, lose our focus, grab the 'power' with a grip of attachment, it's gone. To know the art of knowing is to master this delicate balance. It's a lesson I've been learning over and over again, in all its subtlety.

The next day we met at Theresa's farmhouse at 8 A.M.. to begin the second level initiation. We were told to fast for both days, except for a few pieces of fruit and water to drink. Unlike the first level, we were inside most of the day, learning more specifically about different practices in the tradition. We learned about the different types of energy ('heavy' and 'refined') and how to work with them. We each made our first despacho and were taught more specifically about each element that went into the offering and what it symbolized. We also learned how to "read" coca leaves.

That morning we received our first "energy transmission" from them. Afterwards we were invited to go outside to commune with nature (without speaking with one another.) I had the most beautiful connection with the flowers and Mother Earth. It was akin to the feeling one has when they have just fallen in love with someone, when just being in the other's presence creates a kind of ecstasy. I looked into a flower, held it tenderly with a soft caress and gazed in awe at the beauty, color and complexity of this masterpiece of creation. It was a gentle, lovely, peaceful feeling, quite different than I had ever experienced with plants and flowers.

There were times during the day and night that I felt tired or hungry or physically uncomfortable but mostly I felt open and relaxed, without questions or confusion, simply open to receive what they were offering us. That night we slept on the floor in our sleeping bags and got up early for our second day. It felt like something very significant was happening but my mind wasn't deciphering what it was that felt different.

In the morning we received our second energy 'transmission'. They gave us two symbols to use, to deepen our intuition and our connection with the hanoq pacha (the upper world). After that they introduced us to Thabo, one of Theresa's farm workers. We were asked to use the symbols we had just been given in order to "diagnose" Thabo. We wrote down all our perceptions on a piece of paper.

I saw a 'block' in his lungs and perceived a great sadness in him. I wrote that his 'life force' was blocked, that he had lost his desire to live. I 'saw' some difficult relations in his family. More personal information about his life came to me as I wrote, about what was affecting his health and well-being. Things came to me and I wrote them down but I didn't have any idea if they were correct or if I was making them up. The source of the information was elusive. I wasn't 'thinking' it although I did have a sense of 'knowing' it. But it was not a 'knowing' I had much confidence in because it was coming from a hidden, unfamiliar source.

The odd part was, I didn't have any attachment to whether I was correct or not. When we all finished writing our diagnoses, we sent healing energy to Thabo using our symbols. I was grateful that this healing was being done by the whole group, and not by me alone. Regis and Sergio also worked with him outside after we had finished.

The initiation ended with a final ceremony on top of the sacred mountain where we received the karpay (energy transmission) of Pampa Misayoq. Similar to the rest of my experiences the previous two days, it felt very significant yet I had no way to adequately register why or how it would impact on me in the days, weeks and months to come.

The next two days Sergio lead a Reiki (first level) initiation for about twenty participants, many of whom had also done the workshop. Sally, one of the Pampa Misayoqs, is also a Reiki master and organized this two-day event. So I was able to be a regular participant without any official duties. The meditations we did allowed me to further process what had been happening for me since Regis and Sergio arrived. It also helped me to bring emotional closure and release concerning my imminent departure from South Africa.

In the last meditation we did, I saw myself as an eagle flying over southern Africa. I saw my Johannesburg home far below growing smaller and smaller. I stayed for a while not wanting to leave but then the scene shifted and I was a condor flying over central Peru. I saw the snow covered peaks of Cusco's Ausangate mountain. And then I saw Cusco. I was flooded with emotion at the sight of the city. Tears streamed down my cheeks as I recognized Cusco as my place of origin. I was coming home! It was an extraordinary revelation.

When I came out of the meditation, I kept with me that sense of Cusco as my home—not just my home-to-be but truly a returning. It made sense to me now in a way it hadn't before. All that was happening was enabling me to complete this phase of my life/work and move to the next place, a place that had been patiently awaiting my return. I remembered again the psychic in New York who told me in 1987, "I see you in Peru."

Ten days later, I was on my way.

Are You Wondering?

How were you and the others expected to know what was wrong with Thabo?

Part of the second level initiation is about awakening our perceptions for diagnosis and healing. The symbols we were given opened our intuition and our ability to perceive energetically rather than to know something intellectually. It was a test or an exercise to see the level of this opening in each of us and our natural intuitive ability to see and know with our heart, our soul, and our "third eye". It was really about learning to trust this other way of knowing. For me, doing the diagnosis of Thabo was very liberating because I wasn't invested in being right or wrong. I just wrote whatever came to me. It was interesting to observe what I "saw" without analyzing it. Afterwards we energetically sent him healing. I had more faith in that process than in my diagnosis. Whatever was wrong with him, I knew that the divine love and light we were sending would help him.

When you recognized Cusco in your meditation, did you mean it was your place of origin in a previous life? Do you believe in reincarnation?

Yes, I believe in reincarnation. I believe that your soul never dies, that you live many lives but keep the same soul. With each life, you have experiences that sometimes effect what happens in your next life, things you have to compensate for if you want to grow, if you want to expand your understanding of what it means to be alive. People that study past lives (I am not an authority!) say that you reincarnate in groups or clusters, so that when you meet people with whom you feel a strong connection, it is probable that you knew them in another life, including your family members.

In my meditation I recognized Cusco from a previous lifetime when I lived here. In fact, it is possible that I had more than one lifetime in this area. It was wonderful to feel that sense of "coming home" when I moved to Cusco. It was a sense of belonging despite the fact that I was a foreigner. Past life experiences can sometimes help us in this life but also they can be a distraction from what we came here to do in this lifetime. The most important life is the life you are living right now. Once I was living in Cusco, I needed to stay centered in the present in order to discover why I was here and what I needed to do. This is an ongoing process.

Whether you believe in reincarnation or you believe that one life is all you will have, it is important to make the best of this life. We are all alive at a very special time, a time of big and important change. Whether you believe you chose to be alive at this moment or it was just by chance doesn't really matter. You have the opportunity to choose now whether or not you want to actively contribute to this new awakening in a positive way.

Try This

Sit in a comfortable position, close your eyes and relax. Breathe deeply, in and out. Give thanks for the life you have been given, for everything that has brought you to this moment. Give thanks for all your blessings and for all the challenges you have gone through, for all the things you have learned. As you review your life, see the pattern, the through-line, the tapestry. See the beauty amidst the complexity. Ask for clarity in the present circumstances. Ask for guidance and grace as you search for direction, meaning and purpose. Listen for clarity and guidance

Chapter 17: The Gifts of the Millennium

My last ten days in South Africa were filled with the emotional ups and downs of a person leaving nine years of work and friends behind. I had fashioned a mantra for myself and repeated daily, "I am moving easily through the wonderful changes in my life." Most days this was actually true.

And some days, I was stuck in my old insecurities. I had decided to go to Peru for the new Millennium when I was first there in June '98. The same people that planned the conference where I met Regis and Sergio had organized a one-week Millennium Journey. I had received their registration material, which said deposits had to be sent by June. I had hoped that Regis or Sergio would also be going, but Sergio was vague about his plans and Regis was clear that he would be with his family. I had no idea how difficult it would be to get a hotel or what sort of price-gouging there might be for those days so instead of waiting for plans to materialize with Regis and Sergio, I sent in my money.

My ticket from South Africa to Lima was for December 22nd and I needed to be in Cusco by the 28th for the Millennium Journey. During their stay in South Africa, Sergio had told me that when I arrived in Lima, I was welcome to stay in his house with him and his mother. So I thought I could go to Lima and spend the night at Sergio's then figure out what to do next. If I didn't like Lima surely I could go to Cusco and find something to do for the five days.

I said goodbye to most everyone in Johannesburg rather easily. There were hugs and kisses and best wishes at parties, clubs, and classes. I took it all in on a very even keel with an easy sort of grace. My last Sunday service at St. George's was different though.

irginia, a woman who had been part of our healing group from the beginning stood up. Her life had changed dramatically from being a homeless single mother to being an accomplished actress in a thriving theater company. She sang a song of gratitude she had written for me. There were other songs, poems, and testimonials from people whose lives had been touched by mine. It was very moving. When finally I stood to speak, I thanked them all for the healing and wisdom they had given me and promised that they would forever be in my heart.

And then, I was gone. The house got packed, the car got sold, everything got done and I was on a plane headed for my first stop, Buenos Aries. By December 23rd I was sitting in my guest apartment at Sergio's house in Lima overlooking a beautiful back yard garden. Sergio had met me at the airport in the early hours of the morning. I was pleased to learn that he had decided to go to Cusco himself for the Millennium. He had just gotten a ticket from a friend for the 28th. He was a bit distressed to learn that I did not yet have a ticket for Cusco. All the flights, he told me, were booked until January 4th! Instead of panicking, I thought "Oh, well... Maybe he can get me a ticket on the flight he's on. With Sergio and God, anything is possible." Sure enough, after a lovely few days in Lima with Sergio and his mother, Maria, a ticket materialized and when we checked in we were both given first class seats!

One evening while we were still in Lima, some friends of Sergio's came over. One of them mentioned it was relatively inexpensive to live in Cusco. "Good," I said, "then maybe I can afford to live there without an income." To which Sergio replied, "You can work there."

"Doing what?" I asked.

"You can do healing work. You can charge for that. With a few clients a day, you can make enough money to live." This was the second time that he or Regis had mentioned my ability to heal and it was beginning to sink in that this might really be a possibility for me.

I began to want more time with Sergio to learn from him. I thought it would be more important to enter the new year and the new millennium with him than with the program I had booked back in June. I regretted my lack of trust that I might be able to spend this important time with Sergio. We went out to dinner the evening before our flight to Cusco and I told him, I'd really rather be with him than do the trip I had booked. I didn't even mind losing the money I'd paid for it. Sergio told me that was not possible, that he needed some time alone but perhaps we would have a few days together after the New Year.

As we drove around Lima after dinner, I asked him what he thought of me. He told me I was smart, practical, and had an open heart. But then he said, "You have some spiritual gifts, but you also get caught in the material realm and it takes you away from the spiritual path."

I got another lesson the next day in Cusco when I made some teasing, sarcastic remark to Sergio and he quickly replied. "Why do you say such rubbish? You waste your energy when you do such things." Immediately I became conscious of the stirred up emotions I was feeling because I was about to go off with this new group of people. I knew his reprimand was a warning to stay centered in myself. For once my ego was grateful rather than defensive and I thanked him for helping me. It is so true that even the smallest of power plays puts you back in the material realm and cuts you off from real power, the power of love.

I asked him again if I could be with him that week, and again he said no. "You did not trust that what was yours would come to you," he told me. "Now you have put things into motion that must be played out. That is the law." I felt disheartened and he must have seen that for he next said, "You will receive three things during this week. Watch for them." He would say no more about what those things were. We said good-bye as I boarded the bus to Pisac with the rest of our Millennium group. He said he would come to Raqchi for our ceremony there in two days.

After we arrived in Pisac, I took a walk up to the top of the terrace at the hotel. Another woman who was with the group came up shortly after me. We had a wonderful, connected conversation. She was an author and she told me her publisher, Grace, was also here with the Millennium group. Immediately, I had the sense that Grace would publish the book I was planning to write. Could this be one of the three gifts of which Sergio spoke?

The book. I had written a book two years earlier about people from the outreach ministry in South Africa at the suggestion of a publisher there. Unfortunately, by the time I finished the manuscript, the publishing house had closed their office in Johannesburg. I had sent the book to some other publishers but nothing had come of it. When Regis and Sergio first visited South Africa in January '99, I had asked Sergio if my book would be published. "Well, yes," he had told me, "but your second book will be more successful."

I had never considered writing a second book and didn't know what he was talking about. I had forgotten the conversation until their recent visit. During the Reiki initiation, I had a vision of myself writing a book about my experiences since meeting Regis and Sergio. In my vision, I was writing the book with my best friend, Wendy. The day after that meditation I was talking with Regis and out of nowhere he had said, "You must write a book about your experiences." It seemed the pieces were falling together. Though I hadn't spoken to Wendy about the idea, I knew somehow she would accept. Now, here, in Peru, at this very gathering was a publisher who handled exactly the kind of book I would write. This trip was becoming more interesting by the moment.

I awoke at 5:30 the next morning to do my Reiki practice before the group trip to Machu Picchu. I tried to imagine myself doing healing work in Cusco but it seemed a stretch for me. However, it was my intention to follow the spiritual path in total trust and to be open to all the ways to serve my highest self and all of humanity. I would be patient and knew I would be shown the way.

The bus came at about 7 to take us to Ollantaytambo where we would wait for the train. My impression as we rode along was that North Americans talk way too much. I was content to sit silently and absorb the incredible beauty of the valley and the mountains around us. At the train station in Ollantaytambo, Jose, one of the organizers told me that property in the valley was less than in Cusco, but still more than I had been led to believe by others. I was beginning to think about what sort of property we would need for the Centro Espiritual. Perhaps the thing to do was start out with a small piece of property in or near Cusco, then purchase something larger later. "We'll just have to count on the shaman's way to find the right property," I thought.

Machu Picchu was as marvelous as ever, but a bit too crowded for me that day. I enjoyed the mix of archeology and mythology from our guides but longed for something more. The best part of our trip was a ceremony after lunch during which Don Manuel, a legendary Q'ero Shaman in his 90s, blessed us with his mesa. I could feel the power come from this tiny man like a blast of wind. Amazing.

On the train back to Ollantaytambo, I told Jose about my association with Regis and Sergio and our plans for an interfaith spirituality center. Although I had spoken to him before about some of our plans, this time he seemed to understand on a completely different level. He was immediately affirming and supportive and gave me the names of several people in the United States who might be able to help us with organization and fundraising. Amazing.

Later that evening we did a fire ceremony where we each put a stick in the fire in order to release something. For the first time what I chose to release was not some element of my ordinary, everyday life; not fear, a love interest, South Africa, or work. Instead I asked to release the "pull" in myself that sometimes takes me off the path. I had heard Sergio's warning the day before and wanted to integrate that important lesson as quickly as possible. I knew that if it were my intention, it would be done. I had a sense of the great significance of this request for me. Amazing.

The next morning we boarded another bus for Raqchi, a two-hour drive through another beautiful river valley. I felt the energy of the place as soon as we arrived. Raqchi is home to an ancient sacred temple of the Inka, the Wiraqocha Temple. We were there to perform despachos and to cleanse ourselves, not only for our own growth and development, but to create energy that would help call in the next great healers and leaders predicted in the Inka prophecies. I don't think I understood the significance of what we were doing at the time, but I knew the place was something special. We took an archeological tour first and that was very impressive. The temple wall is massive as is the entire complex. I sensed its spiritual power.

Sergio arrived soon after we did, with his friend Ana Maria from Lima. I had met her in Cusco two days before and liked her very much. Now, I found out her family had property in Urubamba that they might want to sell for the Centro Espiritual. I was happy to see both of them again. After our picnic lunch on the lawn, Don Manuel and the other Q'ero shamans prepared to make two despachos right in front of where I was sitting. In a group of fifty or so people I felt blessed that the spot they prepared to make the beautiful offerings was so close. When you sit for a despacho, it is a kind of meditation; no one speaks as the offering is built. The energy that emanates from the shamans and the participants is palpable, and the clearer the intentions of the gathering, the stronger the energy will be.

In this case our energies seemed magnified by our surroundings. We began by cleansing our three centers—head, heart, and belly—in the nearby ritual baths. Then, we returned to our places to meditate while Don Manuel and Don Martine built the despachos. We were invited to place coca leaves signifying our intentions into the bundles and for mine I asked to manifest my new life and calling. An elderly Indian woman, who happened upon our gathering on her way home, came forward to offer coca leaves. She and Don Manuel exchanged words in Quechua as he received her coca leaves and placed them lovingly into the despacho. The despacho is an offering and a chance to send your desires to the Divine Creator. This woman who grew up with the tradition knew not to miss such an opportunity and her simple act of faith reaffirmed for me that what we were doing was rooted solidly in tradition, an ancient practice.

Once the bundles were finished they were wrapped in mantas and we were cleansed with both despachos, as they passed it from our heads down our chests and our backs. I felt transported. All day I had been quiet, observant, and now I felt completely connected to the spiritual energy of the place. I asked Sergio if I could go back to Cusco with him, but he told me I mustn't bypass any of my steps. "Already," he told me, "you have received two things. On the first of January you will receive the third." He spoke to me gently, and I felt he could see that I was in a different space. I was so grateful to have him as my teacher.

Later, I meditated by myself in a round stone structure, luxuriating in the energy there. When finally I returned to the bus, I found everyone had been waiting for me. I had no sense of time in that place, only of peace, love, and joy. I found several perfect heart stones that day, reminding me to love and trust.

When we got back to the hotel, Jose told me there was a man with property south of Cusco whom I could meet. He had some pictures that looked lovely and it sounded as if the property might be right for us. I hoped Sergio would be able to go with me to see it before he went back to Lima.

On one of the stops we made on the way home from Raqchi, I had found a large heart stone, heavy, smooth and flat about 8 inches in diameter. I had it in my hand after I talked with Jose and the man with the property. On the way to my room I noticed one of the Q'ero and showed it to him. He was very impressed, took it from me, blessed it and told me I must put it in my mesa. I was delighted he liked it but it weighed about five pounds and my mesa was already heavy. Maybe the message here was, "The stronger the power, the heavier the load."

From that conversation I moved to a wine reception where I again spoke with the author I met earlier in the trip. This time, Grace, the publisher, was with her. When we were introduced, I felt a strong and lovely connection with this vibrant, intelligent woman. Though I did tell her about my idea for a book and she agreed to take a look at the manuscript of my previous project, I had a feeling that there was more to our being together on this trip than simply for me to meet her. I sensed there would be a mutual exchange between us. I felt she carried some heaviness in her that she needed to release, but I knew when the time was right, I would be able to help her.

At dinner that evening, I overheard Grace talking with another woman and gathered that there was indeed a problem, a relationship issue. That night in my room, I kept thinking of what Regis told me in our first direct conversation when I met him at the Urabamba conference. "Human beings, they do things… they get angry and hurt each other. But that's not what matters. Only love matters." Perhaps Regis' admonition was my gift to Grace in exchange for her reading my manuscript. The principal of reciprocity is central to the Andean tradition. Things work better when both parties gain. I believe it is a major reason why the lives of so many in the United States are filled with activity but devoid of happiness; they work to accumulate for themselves, rarely to exchange with others. I awoke that last day of 1999 full of love and gratitude for my incredible life. I wanted only to be quiet, to focus on the understanding that we must rise above the material and not get "stuck" in the human things we do to one another. Love is the only antidote strong enough to heal the world.

After breakfast, I saw Don Manuel sitting by himself. I greeted him in Spanish and asked if he had enjoyed the dancing I saw him doing the night before. He smiled, said "Yes," then something else that I interpreted as being a sign of recognition that I was on the spiritual path. I thought he was telling me I should keep studying. I wondered as I walked away if it might be possible to have some type of private session with him.

Later in the day I went for a walk not far from the hotel where I found a small stone in the absolutely perfect shape of a heart, then several more. I began to commune with the rocks—their energy calling me from many directions—and I began to find amazing stones of all shapes, colors and sizes, with very unique markings. It seemed everywhere I looked there was another one more fascinating than the last. My hands and pockets were full of fantastic stones as I walked back to the hotel jubilantly. It felt like those rocks had found me. They were like long lost friends, or little leprechauns I had scooped up to carry with me. My joy was barely containable, and when I saw Don Francisco and Don Manuel standing together outside their room, I showed them what I had found.

They seemed quite amazed by the stones, even more than I was. They spoke excitedly to each other in Quechua. Then they motioned for me to come into their room and bring the stones with me. The mood became more reverent. Don Manuel took the stones from me and laid them on a cloth. Then he took three items out of his own mesa and put them on top of my stones. He blessed the stones with his mesa as Don Francisco chanted prayers and blessings. I stood in front of the table where he was working and an energy force sent tingles through my arms and chest it was so strong. It felt like an electrical surge running through my body. I knew Don Manuel was a very powerful shaman. I couldn't quite believe he was using his own mesa to charge my stones, which for some reason seemed to impress him with their power. When his ceremony was finished, he wrapped the stones in a hand-woven Q'ero manta and told me I must put them in my mesa.

A person's mesa must travel with them at all times if they are to stay in their power and mine now weighed about ten pounds! But I knew it was an incredible gift and honor to have had my stones blessed in such a fashion. If Don Manuel said they must go in the mesa, it would be so. I had wanted a private session with Don Manuel, but I had never expected anything like this.

I rebuilt my mesa but had questions about how everything was to be done so when I went to lunch and saw Jose and Don Manuel standing together, I asked my questions and Jose interpreted for us. Then Don Manuel came and sat next to me at lunch. I asked if he could meet with me and he said he would do a coca reading for me later that night.

During the reading, Karina translated for Don Manuel, who only spoke Quechua. He threw the coca leaves on his manta and looked carefully at them before raising his head and saying, "You are very lucky." After another look into the leaves, he asked, "What kind of work do you do?" I told him I had just finished my job but I wanted to do spiritual healing work. "Yes, you will have very good luck with this work. It will go well for you. Have you made a despacho for your new project?" I told him I hadn't yet. "You must make a despacho and then everything will go very well, although it will take some time." I asked if there was other work that I should be doing while the Spirituality Center was being developed. "If you continue to study this tradition, you will become a leader. You will be a healer. You will help many people, physically, emotionally, spiritually. You will heal them. It is good for you to learn more about the Andean tradition in Cusco. I will teach you. You learn things very easily and quickly. You also have a very strong mesa. This will help you."

He paused again and looked down at the coca leaves. "You can also write a book."

Then it was over. Other people had told me about their coca readings that were full of potential romance or warnings of health problems. My reading on the other hand was exactly what seemed to be unfolding in my life. No warnings, no problems. He knew none of the facts about my life and yet he saw everything just the way I wanted it to be. "You are very lucky". Wow, was that an understatement.

When I saw Grace later that evening, I gave her the large heart stone and Regis' words of wisdom. She was very touched and later told me how much it had helped her. After dark there was a fire ceremony led by Don Manuel and the other Q'ero in the park across the street from the hotel, which ended about 10:00 P.M. Everyone went back to the hotel to dress for the big New Year's dinner dance. Many people brought formal attire for the occasion and it was fun to see how different people looked without their hiking boots and t-shirts.

At 11:30 I slipped away to return to the park across the street to sit in quiet meditation for an hour, which Sergio had suggested I do. The embers of our earlier fire were still burning and I put on a few more logs to fuel the flames. I sat in silence, feeling the vibrations of the mountains all around me and the stars sparkling above me. I thought of other New Year's and marveled at my choice to be alone at midnight on this night of nights. I remembered being a teenager thinking it would be so exciting to celebrate the turn of the century and what a party it would be. Being alone under a starry sky enchanted by the mystical Andean peaks was nothing I could have imagined then but it was exactly where I wanted to be now, alone yet totally connected with everything. Just like I was on the swing when I was three.

At 12:30 I went back to the party but never really got into the party atmosphere. I felt such a deep and profound gratitude for my life and all that was happening. Party hats and confetti didn't capture the sentiments I was feeling. I chatted a bit with new friends I had made and then went off to bed, where I continued to reflect on how different my life was now compared to how I had imagined it only a few years earlier.

The things that seemed important to me then were meaningless to me now. One of the dangers of projecting the future is that you cannot possibly conceive a plan as magnificent as the one to which the universe can lead you. But we get stuck in those projections and hold on to them tightly sometimes, not allowing the universe to work its magic. When we learn to trust and to know that power is always working toward our best interests it becomes easier to let go and live in the flow. When we keep our intentions clear, our choices become clear and far simpler than when we are mired in our own machinations, struggling to make things happen.

On this trip, everything was coming to me. I kept thinking of the three things Sergio had promised me. It seemed to me that I'd already passed that number long ago and the gifts just kept piling up. Sometimes it's like that, everything that happens we can receive as a gift. Other times things happen that might also be gifts but we cannot see them at all because they come to us disguised as frustration, disappointment, or hardship. Yet even in those difficult moments we have a choice. We can feel put upon, hurt, angry, rejected or we can look for the gift. Having done it both ways, I can tell you that the second way is easier. Yes, there will still be hurts and disappointments, but you do not carry them around with you for days or months or lifetimes. You no longer get stuck in your emotions, neither the highs nor the lows.

I tell you this now because the Millennium Journey was an incredible high. I have never had so many exciting things happen to me, spiritually and materially, so quickly in my life. The old Diane would have clutched each possibility presented there as a definite, ordained by God, promise of the future. And, I would have been disappointed. Some of the possibilities presented to me on that trip have happened and were more fun and fulfilling than I expected. Some did not happened. Grace, for instance, left publishing before I wrote my manuscript. Others are still yet to be determined. What I do know for sure is that possibilities that do not pan out (no matter how probable they seem at the time,) are replaced without us having to do anything at all, by other possibilities, grander possibilities, magical possibilities.

This doesn't mean that we don't actively participate in what is happening in our lives. In fact, the more present we are able to be, the better equipped we are to allow the universe to assist us in manifesting our desires. In order to be fully present we need to remove the blocks within us that blur our vision. These blocks have many forms: anger, fear, greed, prejudice, self-pity, doubt. As we release these things we are able to fill the empty spaces with gratitude, love, and compassion. This allows us to rise above the need for life to be "fair". It allows us to accept that people hurt us, and that things beyond our comprehension happen. It allows us to experience the power of love and compassion to transform these things and thereby create the possibility for healing and true change.

When we consciously live this way, our reason for being alive becomes clearer and we can begin to live each moment of life, marvelous, miraculous life, with joy and purpose. The Andean path has helped me learn how to live this way. There are also other religious practices and spiritual traditions that help people to live this way. The promise of the Andean tradition, like many others, is that when we learn to be peaceful and loving, we will create a heaven on earth, where every rock, wave, and creature is valued. The harmony and peace foretold in the Andean prophecies is closer than we might think.

If you are reading this book, you know that this is true. Some part of you longs for it, wants to believe it, or is currently doing everything you know to do to achieve it. I used to think it was impossible; how could we get all those people out there to change? And then, I changed. Working with the elements and connecting with alternative ways of knowing, has taught me how to release heavy emotions and replace them with peace and love. I rarely feel the need these days to make people see things my way and I no longer engage in many of the activities that used to sap my energy and make me feel hopeless. I have learned to work with energy, to build it, keep it safe, heal with it and use it wisely. When you learn to live this way—truly in the present, with love for all, conserving and using your energy wisely with conscious intention, you won't want to go back to the old way. You will be transformed. And then the earth and all its inhabitants are one step closer to the golden age, the taripay pacha, the age of meeting yourself again.

Are You Wondering?

Explain the principle of reciprocity—that "things work better when both parties gain".

When there is a reciprocal exchange things are in balance, in harmony. The energy flows freely. It is like an electrical current that produces light. When you take something without giving in return then it cuts the current and the light goes out. There is less energy flowing which creates a metaphorical 'darkness' that affects not only the two people involved but also the environment in which they live. Conversely, when one lives under the principle of anyi then everything becomes an exchange. Before there was money, most communities used a barter system where goods and services were exchanged, to meet the needs of the family and community. This still exists in some high remote communities in the Andes.

With urbanization and modern times, barter-exchange was replaced with buying and selling and working for a salary. Especially in cities, the principal of anyi gets lost. We no longer feel the same connection with people and nature. By paying for something, we believe that we own it without responsibility beyond the exchange of money. This attitude effects how we live our lives. We no longer feel that our quality of life is related to those around us or governed by the laws of nature. We ignore Pachamama because we buy our food in the grocery store. It is only when a natural disaster hits, we are reminded that nature is not within our control.

When I worked with the homeless in South Africa, I could see how much it meant to people in the community just to be heard, to be seen, to be greeted by name. Instead of giving money, I gave people a smile and a warm hello. Almost always, I got a big smile in return. There was something very special about that exchange. It lit up not only our faces but also the environment around us. It was a human exchange where both parties gained something, in the giving and the receiving.

Here where I live in the small town of Pisac, near Cusco, every person you pass greets you. If there are two or three of us walking together, they greet each one of us, "Good morning senora. Good morning, senor. Good morning senora." In Cusco, people greet you but not everyone, all the time. In Lima or New York, I pass the streets anonymously with barely anyone making eye contact.

The art of exchange, of anyi, of reciprocity, needs to be relearned. It takes time and intention and consciousness of our connection with other humans and all of nature.

Try This

At least once a day for a week (or a month) consciously engage in anyi. Offer some form of exchange that takes you out of your normal routine. If you are at the market buying something, in addition to the exchange of money, offer a smile or a greeting. When you eat your meal, make an offering to Pachamama for the harvest. When you turn on the light, think of the sun, the fire element and give thanks for this source of illumination and warmth. Give something (besides money) freely and spontaneously to someone— a flower, an encouraging note, a book you've finished reading. Whenever someone offers you something, receive it graciously. The web of exchange is vast. Become an active participant in it.

What is the function of your mesa and how is it "powerful"?

My mesa is a collection of stones from power places and other sacred objects that have significance to me. It sits on my altar and is with me in all the Andean ceremonies I do. I use it to cleanse heavy energy from people and also to energize and empower them.

The formation of one's mesa is a sacred process that continues during her or his life. One's mesa grows with each level of initiation. Wherever spiritual work is done, that place becomes sacred. The initiate or master selects a stone from that place as a way of honoring the power of the experience as well as the place. There are sites around the world, especially in the Andes where sacred ceremonies have been performed over hundreds, even thousands of years. These places have a high vibration or spiritual energy, which is held in the stones from these places, like a memory. You always ask permission of the stone before removing it, to place it in your mesa. The mesa is wrapped in a bundle with a woven Andean cloth or manta, which protects the objects inside. In this way, the power of the initiations, the ceremonies, the ancient rituals, the spiritual work is held in the mesa and used as a tool for healing and cleansing heavy energy. The masters say, "Your mesa is your power."

Chapter 18: Knowing Is Not Like That

In the days after the Millennium Journey, I stayed in Cusco, spending time with Sergio, Ana Maria, and other newfound friends. I was trying to integrate all the things that had come to me in that fantastic week. On Monday, January 3rd, I went with Sergio to the despacho market, did a bit of exploring, then met Ana Maria at her cousin's cafe in the Plaza de Armas. I got back to the hostel where I was staying in time for a quick nap before Sergio and the property owner Jose had introduced me to in Pisac, came to pick me up. We drove to Andahuaylillas to see the property, which was lovely but too steep to use for the center. At dinner, Sergio told me he was doing a despacho that evening and I would be assisting him. I only had time to run upstairs, grab my poncho and go; not a minute to review my notes to remember the order of things. Panic started to set in as we got nearer to the house where we were to do the despacho. This was my first time assisting in a despacho and Sergio seemed to expect perfection. I felt absolutely inadequate to the task but we got through it. At the end when Sergio had cleansed everyone I tentatively gestured to see if he wanted me to cleanse him. There was an indiscernible light in his eyes as he handed me the despacho for his cleansing. Later, I found out from Regis that a lower-level Pampa Misayoq does not cleanse the energy of the master. Sergio's humble gesture, receiving my offer so graciously, touched me deeply. Afterwards he told me I had done well for the first time. Possibly, he could see that I was being pretty hard on myself for all I didn't know.

Back at my hotel room I showed him the stones that Don Manuel had blessed and Sergio, too, was impressed. One, he thought, had been carved by the Inkas. Another was marked with a Z and I gave that one to him when he admired it. We went through my mesa together and he said it was, indeed, very power-ful, and that I should not add anything else for now. We said goodbye because he was flying back to Lima in the morning.

The next day I prepared all of the elements I needed to make the despacho that Don Manuel told me would insure the success of my new venture. Alone in my room, facing east, I began by placing the flower petals and coca leaves in their proper positions, followed by the other elements. I loved watching the design and colors change and take shape. My intentions were to develop three things: the Centro Espiritual, my own healing powers, and the book. The ceremony took about forty minutes. The offering was full of my gratitude, prayers and petitions and I felt wonder-ful when it was done.

I called Karina, who had translated Don Manuel's coca reading for me, hoping he might be available to help me burn my despa-cho. Don Manuel wasn't home that day but Karina and I drove out to Huasao, a village twenty minutes south of Cusco that was known for its healers and shamans. We found an associate of Don Martine who took us up a steep incline to a concave vertical rock. It was clear this was a sacred place where many other despachos had been burned. He built a small fire and placed my despacho on it. As the flames grew higher Karina and I turned our backs, as the tradition dictates. I could feel the force of the fire behind me, as I drank in the stunning mountain vista. After some time, he told us we could turn around and added that the despacho had been well received.

Then, on the 8th of January, Regis came.

I had seen Regis do many wonderful and amazing things since I first met him at the Urubamba conference a year and a half before. He is an incredible energy worker and can "see" many things about the lives of others. My desire to emulate the way he worked with people was great and I was excited that we were going to have some time together. He was coming to Cusco to spend the weekend with me looking for property for the center. A few days later I would meet him in Arequipa, his hometown, and we would travel to some sacred sites together.

When Regis arrived we went to lunch and he showed me the new plans for the center. It was in the shape of a chakana and magnificent. Regis' son was the architect and the father had communicated his vision to the son in such a way that the drawings themselves seemed to emanate peace and energy. I was very excited about the plans.

Then he told me that I had done very well in my diagnosis of Thabo during our second level initiation. One other person and I were what he called "A" level. We had gotten it right. "Oh, really?" I said with that same mixture of incredulity and acceptance that I felt when he told me he had come to South Africa because of me. When I did the diagnosis, I felt that information was coming from another source, but had no frame of reference to know if I could trust what I was receiving. Here was my confirmation that I could indeed trust in this new way of knowing.

That evening we had dinner with Juan Victor, a Kuraq Akullaq or highest-level shaman like Regis. They were long-time friends. Regis had called him so that we could meet. I had read of Juan in several books about the Andean tradition. He is an anthropologist as well as a Kuraq Akullaq. His father, also an anthropologist, had been the first to document the traditions of the Q'ero who live in villages at 15,000 feet elevation. Because of their isolation high in the Andes, Juan's father discovered that their spiritual and healing traditions had been unpolluted by the Spanish. It was an honor to meet Juan Victor.

As we sat together over dinner, Regis spoke earnestly to Juan Victor about my qualifications, how long he had waited for me to appear, and that he saw the two of us working together for many years all over the world. The two men also joked together with the easy familiarity of people who have much shared experience. Though most of the conversation was in Spanish, Juan would pause now and then to translate for me. Juan then told Regis that he could see I was ready for higher levels and would soon be his colleague rather than his student. Regis seemed content that it should be so. It was a lovely evening and I was both amazed and grateful to be in the company of two such high-level masters.

The next day was spent looking at several pieces of property in the Sacred Valley. When we reached Urubamba we decided to stop by to visit Regis' first master, Hector, who was 97 and lived nearby. Sadly, we were told when we arrived that Hector had died only months before. Regis paid his respects at the grave of this man who had given him so much; love reflected in the depth of his eyes.

Regis left that evening and the next morning I went back to Machu Picchu to meditate and rest in the energy there. That night I had dreams of shamans and symbols but they did not stay with me when I woke. No matter. I was clear that the internal work was being accomplished without need on my part to analyze. I was grateful.

Gratitude. Such an important aspect of spiritual practice. Gratitude for all that is and gratitude for all that is yet to be. As I meditated the next morning I was grateful for Grace and Wendy helping me with my book, though neither of them had yet said "yes" to the possibility. I knew from using the practice of being grateful beforehand that you are acting creatively when you affirm that these things are so. When you are able to envision them you encourage them to manifest in a way that no amount of wishing or praying for can accomplish. It works with the energy on a different level. It goes outside the realm of what is, to the realm of what is possible.

A few days later I flew to Arequipa and Regis met me at the airport. He arranged for me to stay in a lovely little hotel in Arequipa before we left for Lake Titicaca together. At dinner he talked about my level of spiritual awakening and told me that I was ready for the third level initiation. And one day, he assured me, I would do the fourth level with him, which would mean ten days together on a mountaintop. I remembered Regis' own story of initiation where his incredible gift for seeing and knowing had been activated. It was my intention to be ready when the time came.

Our trip to Lake Titicaca was lighthearted and easy. Regis spoke to me in English and I spoke to him in Spanish and we communicated rather well, even though each of us spoke little of the other's language. It felt like traveling with someone I'd known a very long time; familiar, low-key, fun. Who knew that a spiritual master of such high standing could be such easy company. We had a lovely time together even though the weather was cold and rainy.

One night he told me again that we would be working together for many years to come, traveling to many different places together. I asked him if he had known this when he first met me in Urubamba. "Yes," he replied with a sudden seriousness.

"Well, why," I asked him, "didn't you tell me then, that you were the man I was waiting to meet?"

He looked at me with those dark, loving eyes and I knew I was about to receive a lesson. "Knowing," he told me, "is not like that; if I had told you then, you wouldn't have understood. You were looking for something else at that time. It would only have confused you. You were looking for a husband, not a teacher. I love you, but not with a romantic kind of love. Besides, we both had to choose if we wanted to work together. Now I think you understand this better."

It was true. At the time, I was looking for a special person with whom I shared a destiny. I presumed he would be the man I would marry. I had said yes to that divine voice speaking to me in the jungle: Yes, I wanted to meet the wise man who would be at the conference; the one who would find me, the one who would teach me many things and love me very much. If Regis had told me then, what I knew now, I would have misunderstood or said 'no thanks' because it wasn't what I was expecting.

I was looking for a soul mate and a partner on my spiritual journey. Now I realized that was exactly what I found. I could see that now, because I had begun my journey on the Andean path. I had chosen to move to Peru and help Regis develop the Centro Espiritual. In the jungle, I had said yes to more than I imagined at the time. I had said yes to that inner longing I'd had since childhood, to discover not simply my soul mate but the wisdom, knowledge and expanded consciousness he could teach me to access.

Now I understood that "knowing" is something one does in stages and with each step, we have the option to say yes or no or not now or maybe later. In the past, I had often made decisions based on my "inner knowing" and then sometimes been frustrated and angry if things didn't go the way I thought they should. I'd feel cheated or betrayed by life or my instincts. Here Regis was telling me that when you see a future probability, there are still choices that have to be made; if you say yes, you have to take responsibility for your choice. The way may not always be easy even when you make good choices. You can also say "No," to those things that might be in your best interest. It's up to you. But it is also dependent on the choices of every life that impacts yours.

Perhaps this is why even the most psychic and intuitive among us is sometimes wrong. Someone, somewhere in the necessary chain of events said, "No." This is why the shaman does not often talk about knowing the future but rather, what is probable. The work a shaman does can shift energy so events that were highly improbable are now possible and even probable. Understanding this released me from the need to have things turn out the way I predict or want. Yes, I could intuit that things could or should happen a certain way, but now instead of being frustrated when they didn't, I would be able to respond with a sense of wonder. "Oh," I'd tell myself, "it didn't happen the easy way. Then it will have to happen some other way. I wonder what it will be."

This somehow was the missing piece for me. You could know what was probable but you did not need to be attached to what actually happened because there were too many variables. You could trust that the universe was working on your behalf no matter what was happening on the surface. And you could be grateful for everything; every twist and turn a part of the grand adventure.

I was happy though, that what I was told in the jungle turned out to be true, different than I expected but more than I hoped for.

In the rest of our travels together and particularly our trips to Island of the Sun and Island of the Moon I reflected on this beautiful lesson. When he left Copacabana for Puno and I went in the other direction to La Paz, there were tears in our eyes. I would miss him in the next six months, but I knew all he had taught me would continue to guide me. And it did. Especially in what happened next.

Are You Wondering?

Why can't you watch a despacho being burned?

The masters say that there is a powerful energy and force that is emitted from the despacho as it burns. To watch it burn is therefore dangerous except for the highest-level masters who know how to manage this energy. It is also a type of respect, a tradition that is part of the ceremony.

Explain the levels of the priesthood in the Andean Tradition.

The first level is called paco, which simply means priest. Regis and Sergio use this term for first level initiates who begin the process of learning to work with the elements and to form their mesa. At this level pacos work primarily on themselves, to expand their own consciousness.

The second level is called Pampa Misayoc. At this level you learn to make despachos, read coca leaves and do energy healing, in service to your immediate community. Pampa misayocs act as a conduit on behalf of others who want healing or assistance with some problem or concern.

The third level is Alto Misayoc, the beginning of mastery. It has three grades: ayllu alto misayoc, llaqta alto misayoc and suyu alto misayoc. With each of these grades the master incorporates the power of higher-level apus (mountain spirit energy). With each level new skills and ceremonies are learned. Techniques are taught for healing with herbs, plants, clay, stones and energy. Alto misayocs work with people that come to them from many places, not just their own community.

The forth (and currently highest) level is Kuraq Akulleq, which means "elder chewer of coca leaves". Kuraqs have the power not only to work with the elements and the highest apus, but also with cosmic and planetary forces. Often, like Regis, they are seers and powerful healers. Their community is global.

Chapter 19: The Message is Clear

I returned to Lima with only a few days left before my return to New York and the final six months of my contract with Global Ministries. Ana Maria, Sergio's friend whom I met in Cusco, had agreed to take me shopping for blue jeans in Gamara, a wild part of Lima that is New York's garment district, Filene's Basement, and Hong Kong's Stanley market all rolled into one. We got back to her house for lunch and learned that her friend, Brother Thomas, was coming to join us. Thomas, who she met during her Reiki initiation with Sergio, is nearly blind but has a clear inner vision. He is a Catholic brother who does healing and counseling in the parish where he lives.

Thomas was delightful, and charmed me with his English. He was on his way to visit a 26-year-old in the hospital who was very sick with bone cancer, but he decided to come visit with us first. We enjoyed our lunch, telling each other stories about ourselves. As desert was served, Thomas' cell phone rang. Someone was on the way over but I didn't understand the Spanish explanation of who was coming or why. I had the impression the person was picking up Thomas to drive him to his next appointment.

Soon a big, burley, handsome man arrived. Francisco sat down to join us at the table in the garden and asked Ana Maria for a drink—something alcoholic. He spoke only Spanish. I watched him speak jovially without understanding much of what he was saying or who he was. I noticed that he was a bit drunk. Then, it occurred to me that he might be the father of the young man who was sick. I used the symbols we had been given in our second initiation and felt a growing compassion for the man. I could feel his sadness even as he laughed and joked with Ana Maria and Thomas in Spanish. I could feel the block in his heart center.

They began to talk about his son, Paco, in the hospital, and the rest of his family. I picked up that there were two other children 24, and 18. The more I watched him, and listened to the emotions behind his words, the clearer sense I was getting about the sons and his relations with them. I had a very strong sense that the youngest son was having a very difficult time. I said to Francisco (with Ana Maria translating), "It's important for you to talk to your sons about what is happening, especially to the younger one. They need to "feel" what is happening and express it."

He responded in a flurry of Spanish, which I didn't understand. Ana Maria and Thomas were engaged in conversation with him, so I continued to listen and observe, ignoring the words and honing in on what I was "seeing". I became more and more clear that the younger son was in trouble and that the father needed to speak to him. It was such a strong feeling that I interrupted and asked Ana Maria to translate. Then the connection between Francisco and me became stronger. He looked directly at me as he told me his younger son wouldn't speak about what was happening to his brother. I told him it was important.

Then Thomas turned to me and said, "I have met Alvero and I agree with you that he is not well. Are you a clairvoyant?" I was a bit stunned by the question but heard myself answer, "Yes, sometimes." Clairvoyant or not, I knew what I was sensing was true and I also felt a sense of urgency to communicate this to Francisco. Ana Maria then told me that no one had told Paco about the seriousness of his condition, that he was dying. In fact, they had instructed the doctors to tell him nothing for fear the news would upset him. Again, I spoke directly to Francisco.

"It is very important that you talk with Paco, alone, just the two of you. Tell him the truth about his condition, not for him because he already knows, but for you. If you can do this, it will free Paco, who will in turn tell you something very special and important that he has been waiting to tell you. This can only happen if you can speak the truth to him while you are sober." I don't know how I knew these things but it was as clear as a bell to me that my task was to communicate this to Francisco with as much urgency as possible.

"I am afraid to tell him. He is a very sensitive boy. What if I'm wrong? What if it is not the right thing to do?"

"The biggest gift you can give your son," I responded, "the most loving thing you can do for him, is to speak with him openly. First you must speak with Paco, just the two of you. Then speak with Alvero, just the two of you. Then Alvero and Paco will be able to speak because they also have some things they need to say to each other. Do this soon because Paco doesn't have much more time."

"If I do this will he get better?"

"No," I said as gently as I could. "This is an opportunity for you. It will free Paco to die peacefully. You have a gift to give Paco and he has a gift to give you."

The connection between the two of us was very strong now. It was as if we were bound by some invisible cord from a source beyond us both. I could feel Francisco's fear but I knew he recognized what I was saying as the truth. The only question was how he could move beyond his own fear to seize this opportunity. I could feel his highest self ready to respond and his weaker self only wanting to hide in another glass of whiskey.

"Can you come and visit Paco in the hospital?" he implored as if somehow I could fix everything.

"I am returning to New York tomorrow but I would be happy to go with you now or come in the morning. Where is Alvero?" I felt strongly that he was the one in the most danger. I knew that Paco had already made peace with his passing. I also felt that his mother was distraught but was dealing with her emotions and would be able to handle what was happening. So was his sister. The unfinished business was between father and sons. I could see the whole family clearly and could feel what each one was feeling.

He wrote down my name and the phone number at Sergio's. "What do you do?" he asked.

"I'm a minister, pastora, and also a healer."

"I need to talk with my wife about this."

"Yes, it will be good to talk with her because she will understand this. But when you speak with Paco, you should be alone with him." I felt the emotional strength of his wife and how much he depended on her.

He looked directly at me, his eyes pleading for help. "What would you say to my son if you were me?"

The compassion I felt for him was so full I thought my heart would burst. "You will know how to speak to your son. All the right words will come to you. Trust your heart." Then I added, "I could be in the room with you if that would help you."

"No. No. Tomorrow is too soon. I need to discuss it with my wife. It will take some time. But I'll call you in the morning. Perhaps you can talk with my wife. She speaks English." I could feel the battle raging inside him; the part that wanted to connect with his son in this special way and the part that just couldn't bear the thought of telling his son he was dying, for then he would have to believe it himself.

All I could do was send him love and hope he would overcome his fear. The choice was his to make. Finally he stood up to leave and gave me a big hug. He said he could feel the strength of my energy. I could feel his sorrow and his fear like a dense black ball in his chest and knew if he didn't release it soon, he too would be sick.

With tears welling up in his eyes, he said, "I prayed to let the cancer pass to me, if it would heal my son."

I choked back my own tears and said, "It's not necessary. Just trust your heart and speak to your son."

We hugged again and he gave me his card, saying he would meditate on it that night and maybe call in the morning. Maybe. I promised that I would hold all of them in my thoughts and prayers.

"I know that I came to this house today for a reason." he said and we all agreed. He thanked me as we said our last goodbyes, then he left with Thomas.

Ana Maria and I didn't speak for a while. I had no words to explain what happened or how I knew what I knew. But there was no doubt at all that everything I told him and all that I "saw" was true. I felt only awe for the insight I had been given, the message spoken through me. It was different from the diagnosis I did on Thabo at Theresa's farm. Even though I had been "100%" right according to Regis and Sergio, I didn't know I was right. This time I knew. I knew the whole family without ever meeting any of them but the father.

The cord that connected me to Francisco remained in place even after I returned to New York. He didn't phone me at Sergio's. Every day I visualized him and his family surrounded by light and love but as each day passed, I could sense that he was unable to speak with his sons. Then one day about three weeks later, I felt the cord break and knew Paco had died. I also knew that no one had spoken to him.

A week later I received an email from Ana Maria confirming that Paco had died on the day I felt it. Her son's girlfriend was the sister of Paco's girlfriend and this was how she knew that no one had spoken to him about his condition. Neither Ana Maria nor Thomas had spoken to Francisco but I could sense he was deep into an alcoholic stupor. I felt a great sadness for the opportunity missed but I knew that my part was only to share with him the information and allow him to choose for himself how to deal with it.

I was reminded that fear is a very toxic substance within us and vowed always to release my own as soon as I became conscious of it. The whole experience with Francisco and what I was able to see and know left me with a renewed sense of awe for what is possible. I realized that whether someone is "healed" or not is beside the point. Each of us every day has the option to choose life, to choose a new way of being, a healthier, happier way of being or not. There is no judgment or condemnation, no right or wrong, only possibilities.

To know is to broaden the options from which we can choose—to reach the place where the possibilities are grand and not mundane. This is the point. This is the power of "to know".

Are You Wondering?

What is the significance of the symbols you use?

During the second and third level initiations, I received symbols, which can be used to enhance my power of perception and manifestation. Each symbol has its unique purpose but all of them are utilized to assist with the task at hand, such as healing, releasing heavy energy, awakening perception and vision, or manifesting a desired outcome. The symbols are secret and not to be used without much respect and consciousness for the power they hold. The more you use them, the more powerful they become for the user. They are both a gift and a responsibility, to be used with intention and awareness.

Do you think it is always good to talk about death with a person who is dying?

If you are centered and calm about the process of dying, then speaking with someone who is dying can be one of the deepest and most amazing experiences of life. Many people who are dying sense that death is close at hand. They sometimes have a lot to process about the lives they led and it is a gift to have a loving friend or relative close by to witness with them. Their processing may be completely internal and you may never hear a word of it, but being there with compassion and love in your heart can liberate them to do what is necessary to release this life peacefully.

It is usually the people who are living that struggle the most with the impending death of a loved one. When you can talk about it, then both the living and the dying have an opportunity to share their feelings and speak of things previously unspoken. Wounds heal, hearts mend, love triumphs over pettiness. Everything is put in perspective.

Death is a natural part of life. It cannot be avoided or wished away. The more consciously we engage in the process and the more present we are, the deeper the insights we can glean from the experience.

Wendy had the opportunity recently to be with her mother, Stig, in the last five days of her life. It was difficult and sometimes exhausting but also very meaningful, an experience she wouldn't have missed for anything. Stig had been living with cancer for more than 14 years and had been in hospice care for two years. Though she was in and out of consciousness at the end, there were special moments with her children and grandchildren that Wendy was grateful to witness, moments of rare beauty and deep love.

At one point in those five days, Wendy was in her mother's room, tidying up while her mother slept. She noticed a sheet of paper on a chest tucked under some books and felt compelled to pull it out and see what it was. On the page was one of her mother's favorite old hymns, one that Wendy and Stig had sung many times with the church choir they both belonged to in Wendy's youth. One of the grandchildren, Eric, walked in and quietly asked what she was reading. "It's one of Grannie's favorite songs," she told him, "In the Garden." When Eric responded that he didn't know the song, Wendy began to softly sing, reading the words from the page, words of grace and comfort. Then, from the bed, in a tiny voice, came the sound of her mother singing along. The softest smile was on her face, a smile that spoke of love and memories and pleasure. They sang together as they had so many years before, holding hands, sharing joy and sadness, love and tears. So many messages given and received unspoken and unconditional through a song.

There is so much to be lost, if you don't engage the process of dying. To be with a loved one who is dying is a privilege and a special opportunity that should not be missed. Put aside your fear and trust in divine grace. Be present, loving and honest and all the right words (or songs) will come.

TO KNOW

To know something, in the Andean Tradition, is to understand it through experience, not simply intellectually. It is a wisdom born of practice. It is a knowing so big that the mind cannot contain it. This knowledge is held in the heart and the soul and the cosmos, beyond time and space, not only in the mind. As your consciousness expands, so does your capacity to perceive, to intuit, to process and to experience life on a grand scale.

Imagine that your ability to know is like a television set. You grow up, you go to school, you learn things. You are plugged in and you have the three main network channels. You think that is all there is. Then you get older and you hear about alternative channels. You go looking for better reception. You put up an antenna and soon you are getting 12 channels instead of three. You realize there is much more information out there than you previously knew about. It is exciting. You are learning, you are growing, you are expanding your awareness.

More possibilities exist. But it doesn't stop there because the more you learn, the more you want to know. Soon you are hooked up to cable and you are getting hundreds of channels. Now you have to choose, you have to discern. You have to use the information available to you to discover the path you want to follow – to discover what is illuminating and what is constricting.

As you amplify your consciousness, the vibration becomes higher. You filter out the lower frequencies and you tune in to the more refined, the more subtle. You program your own selections. You start downloading from a satellite. From that distance out in space, the frequencies can travel around the globe from the same source. But you need a special "dish" to receive the information, for it to broadcast to you loud and clear.

This tradition teaches you how to receive this refined information, how to build your reception dish. And more importantly how to process the information you receive into knowledge and wisdom, through practice and experience.

You learn to know by using all your senses, by connecting with the elements and the forces of nature. You expand your awareness through meditation, visualization, concentration and listening with an open mind and heart. You learn to be present to every moment. As you release your heavy energy (lower frequencies) you clear space for finer energy, better reception.

It is a never-ending process of clearing, cleaning, maintaining, expanding, processing, fine-tuning and amplifying. Learn and grow. Manifest the possibilities and more and more present themselves. This is what it means to know.

SECTION FIVE:
TO BE SILENT

Chapter 20: The Ways of Water

To Be Silent. It may sound like there is not much to it. Deceptively simple. Yet silence is the place where the most happens. I believe you can approach the four sacred words of the tradition in any order but without silence, daring lacks intention, wanting lacks consciousness, and there is no path to access other ways of knowing. You can want before you have the courage to dare, or know something is so before you ever realize you want it. But silence is always central, the most necessary ingredient for self-discovery and transformation.

Without silence there is no integration of your spiritual practice into your everyday existence. You can have a mystical mountaintop experience, but if you do not learn how to quiet your mind and listen, the wisdom gained from that moment will evaporate as you deal with the difficulties and frustrations of being human. You simply cannot know the other ways of knowing without silence and stillness.

In the Andean tradition, water is the element that corresponds with the sacred word To Be Silent. The planet earth is mostly water, and so are our physical bodies. Our body chemistry is an inextricable link to the planet herself. Like the blood in our veins, the earth's water nourishes all her inhabitants. The currents and rhythms of water pulse through our bodies and enable us to feel connected with everyone and everything.

Water is a solvent, a cleaning agent in the material world. So it is in the spiritual world as well. When we engage with water, staring at a river or the ocean, swimming peacefully in a pool, we are being cleansed. All our sadness, anger, hostility, stress can dissolve away in the water. We become rebalanced because water is always in balance. If you're thinking, "Gee, the last time I took my family to the beach

I didn't return feeling very balanced," then you probably didn't really engage the water. Perhaps your consciousness was with the food, the car, the beach house and all the other practical details.

When working with the elements, it is important to be conscious and fully present with your intention to connect. All the Andean practices with the elements happen in silence. If we want to learn what the elements know, we have to listen and being silent helps us listen. We can release our anger or hurt to the earth or a tree and afterwards feel refreshed, centered. We can use the fire of the sun to increase our energy, vitality, and focus. Air, can transport us, opening our minds, broadening our vision, and connecting us to the cosmos. Water can cleanse and balance us. Water and silence, slow us down. You know this if you've ever snorkeled or scuba-dived. Surrounded by form-fitting liquid you float in a world moving in slow motion, you hear your breath and the beat of your heart. You slow down to match your surroundings.

This is also one of the properties of water. It takes on the shape of its container. Imagine the water in a raging river. Put that water in a glass and it becomes still and level. Tip the glass at an angle and the water again finds horizontal. Move it to a different container, the same thing happens. Put it back in the river and it picks up the current moving just as fast as the water around it. No matter where it goes, it adapts and is always seeking balance.

Learning from the water, we too can adapt to all situations and stay balanced. In silence, we unblock our energy channels, which allows us to tune in to higher frequencies; to live life calmer and more connected. As we release our heavy emotions, we find we have more time and energy to complete tasks. Prioritizing becomes simpler for we no longer feel pressured by the expectations of others. When we cultivate silence, we begin to ask what is right for us in the moment and live more fully in the present.

And the present is the place where transformation happens.

Try This

When you are at the beach, take at least twenty minutes with no other task than to watch the water and breathe. You may, at first, run through the litany of things to be done, but if you stay and gently, gently turn your focus to the water, all of those things will float away in the water's current. You will be left with a peacefulness that enables you to be present to your life in a new way, not merely running through it, checking off tasks on your list.

Try This

When you can't get to the ocean or a river, there is a wonderful exercise you can do in the shower. The point is to release heaviness and let the water move it away from you. In the shower, allow the water to wash over you and become aware that you are cleansing your energy field, not just your body. Let all of your tensions, frustrations, and worries dissolve and melt down the drain. If you have taken on the heavy emotions of others, wash them away as well. Be conscious of the water, the way it looks, feels, smells. Thank the water for helping you in this way.

Try This

When you step out of the shower, you are clean and your energy field is clean. This means that you are also vulnerable, so you want to seal your energy field to give yourself some protection from heavy energies that bombard you through the day. First, affirm who you are, the fabulous you that you know exists, then repeat three times. "I know who I am. Nothing and no one can change this." As you repeat these words imagine the light of Divine love putting protection around you, a golden shield or bubble that radiates love and reflects love back to people even if what they send your way is heavy energy.

Chapter 21: Balance

When Regis and Sergio first spoke to me about not getting stuck in my emotions, I didn't really understand why my emotional responses were so problematic to them. I'd always been a person who expressed my emotions freely whether they were anger, frustration, joy or elation. I had always considered this a reasonably healthy thing. During the first Inka workshop however, I was able to recognize how sometimes my emotions were preventing me from accessing the other ways of knowing that they were teaching us. When we are focused on our emotions, we are firmly anchored in the material realm. Those emotions can feel like they are outside invaders taking control of us.

That kind of invasive-feeling emotion I call an "ego-based" emotion. Generally, it is prompted by outside stimulus—positive or negative. Ego-based emotions are the ones that feel like some part of our 'self' has been rewarded or injured by someone else's behavior. The more attached we are to the hoped-for outcome of a situation, the stronger our emotions will be when our expectation is either met or frustrated.

Often we are not conscious that we have an expectation, or that we have a choice in how we respond emotionally. So, being present and aware of these things is the first step toward not getting stuck in our emotions. When someone does something to us that feels hurtful, it is useful to remember that we have some choices. The more we focus our attention on the other person or the situation, the more likely we are to get stuck. Rather, if we take a few deep breaths, it will help re-center our energy within us. What keeps us stuck in the emotion, is our desire to change the other person or the situation into our desire or expectation.

A side effect of getting stuck in our emotions is that we give our power away to the other person or to the situation, which only increases our sense of pain, sadness, or frustration. In fact, we can also get stuck in our "positive" emotions which means that we are still at the mercy of outside circumstances. When we lose our center, our power, we are no longer fully present but riding high (or low) on a wave of emotion that is firmly attached to an expectation.

It feels like circumstances are controlling us, as well as our emotional responses to them. Life happens and we have to deal with the fallout emotionally and physically. It's as if we are wearing blinders and can see no possibilities beyond our narrow scope. We lose our connection to the divine source and become out of balance. But there are alternatives. We can change our realities by making that our conscious intention.

In the years since I began studying with Regis and Sergio, I have become more conscious of when my ego-based emotions get activated. Then I do the practices that I know are helpful to release the heavy energy created by these emotions. I don't stay stuck for very long.

I know I have become much calmer since consciously practicing these things. But in March of 2001, I became aware of another aspect of emotional imbalance and why it can be problematic, even potentially dangerous. Regis and I traveled back from Peru to Johannesburg to do another workshop together. Sergio was unable to come so I was assisting Regis without feeling totally adequate to the task. The day the workshop was beginning, we arrived late to the conference center and preparation of all our materials was quite hectic. Participants had arrived before us and some were wandering around the large rustic property.

I was rushing from the conference room to the cottage where Regis was staying, when I saw a woman also walking in the direction of his cottage. I told her not to go that way. She shyly replied she was looking for her room and must be a bit lost. "Well, it's not in this direction," I said curtly and rushed off to see Regis, unaware of the effect I had on her.

My friend Suzan, who helped organize the workshop, had told me about Jackie, a Catholic nun she knew well who was participating. Suzan knew about my Catholic background and thought Jackie and I would enjoy meeting each other. After the first session, she pointed Jackie out to me. I was waiting for an opportunity to connect with her but she always seemed a bit reticent. So instead I worked with her energetically during our meditations.

The third day of the workshop, Regis asked me to speak about the element Air. Before we left Peru, I had been working on the "To Know" section of this book so I felt quite a connection to the topic. It was one of those times when I was present and open and the words just flowed out of me. I hadn't had time to prepare a speech so I spoke from my heart with a passion that was contagious. The eyes of all fifty participants were on me and I could see they caught the flame of my enthusiasm.

Regis said a few words after I finished, then invited everyone to get up and hug one another. Many people came to me and told me how special I am and how I glowed with a loving radiance. They said they could feel the love shinning out of me as I spoke.

The next and last day of the workshop Regis spoke about Fire, its love and passion. He spoke about the power and force of Fire, its alchemy, its strength to transmute. He also warned that because of its intensity, there must always be balance. When he finished he once again invited the participants to stand up and hug one another, to express the love within them. As I hugged Jackie, I told her I had been sending her love and light throughout the workshop. She stepped back a little and said, "You know I almost left after what you said to me the first day." I wasn't sure what she meant and then it came to me that Jackie was the one with whom I was so short in the midst of my own emotional preoccupations.

"Oh Jackie, I am very sorry. I was so stressed out trying to get everything ready." She accepted my apology gracefully and said, "I just needed to tell you." I felt horrible. So many people were telling me how wonderful and loving I was yet Jackie had experienced quite another side of me and that one brief encounter had colored her whole experience of the workshop. Many other people engaged me in conversation after that but I couldn't stop thinking about Jackie. During the break I went to find her. She was sitting alone in a corner of the lawn. She was surprised that I had sought her out and when I asked if I could give her another hug, she seemed touched by the offer.

Again, I told her I was so sorry for what happened, especially because I had been looking forward to getting to know her ever since Suzan told me about her background. "I am an ordained minister but I was raised Catholic. In fact, I was kicked out of my Catholic high school for squirting a nun with a squirt gun. They eventually let me back in. And at my twentieth high school reunion that nun, Sister Ann, came up behind me, spilled her drink on the back of my silk blouse, and said, 'Now we're even'." Jackie laughed in disbelief.

"I don't know why I'm telling you this story but I guess I didn't realize until that time how much I must have hurt Sister Ann for her to still feel that way twenty years later. I really am sorry for being so short with you the other day." Jackie and I hugged again and we both had tears in our eyes. I marveled at how the spirit could turn such an awful situation into such a beautiful healing gift. "The nice part of the story," I told Jackie, "is that at our twenty-fifth reunion, Sister Ann congratulated me on becoming a minister, saying, 'I'm not surprised. You always were a spiritual searcher.' I guess we were both finally able to learn something from the squirt gun experience. Too bad it took so many years."

Later that afternoon, there was a fire to burn the despachos we had made during the workshop. The fire was built log-cabin style with round irregular pieces of wood. It was about four feet high and looked a bit off balance. When the fire ignited it became a giant pillar of flames that shot high into the air. It was awesome to behold. I stared into the flames mesmerized by its heat, power, force. Then a voice came to me that said, "You are like that fire. You have that strength, you have that intensity. That is the power of your love but you need to be responsible to that power and know that your ability to burn people is as strong as your ability to ignite their flames for transformation." I remained transfixed and interconnected with the spirit of the fire. As I watched the despachos beginning to burn, confident they would be well received, the whole blazing pillar toppled, spilling not only the red-hot logs but the contents of the despachos. I gasped in horror.

For a despacho to be received well, the contents must fall into the center of the fire and be totally consumed. Regis, also recognizing the seriousness of what had occurred, walked to the wood-pile and picked up two slender logs. He then began the arduous task of returning every piece of burning wood and each element from the despachos to the center of the fire. I watched in amazement as he matched forces with that blazing intense fire. I could barely tolerate the heat standing five feet away and he was right next to it. Piece by piece, log by log he rescued our offerings and returned them to the fire to be received and consumed.

The message for me was now complete. I knew as clear as day if the foundation of that fire had been in balance from the beginning, it wouldn't have collapsed. It was the intensity of the fire that had tipped it over because it wasn't stable. I recognized the damage it could have done if there wasn't someone there to pick up the pieces before they burned everything around them; someone strong enough, evolved enough to match the force of nature and use that force to restore and transform. I could see how much damage the most loving powerful person could do if not balanced. Then I knew why containing one's emotions is so important.

Working with water, working with Silence keeps us in balance.

Try This
When you get stuck in your emotions, take time to be silent. Breathing deeply can be very helpful in these situations. If you are near a flowing river, you can sit quietly on the bank, staring into the moving water, releasing your emotions into the river, and watching them drift away with the current. If you can't get to a river, then simply put your hands under running water for 5-10 minutes and let the emotions wash down the drain. Be sure to give thanks to the water when you are finished.

Chapter 22: Meditation

So much has been written about the meditative state. It's been studied academically, metaphysically, esoterically, psychologically, neurologically and religiously. Most of you reading this book have at least thought about learning to meditate, if not already involved yourself in some sort of practice. Meditation is an important ingredient for mental, emotional and spiritual well being. Learning to sit in silence matters. Scholars and sages may argue the reasons but I can tell you this much: Without silence there is no integration of your spiritual practice into your everyday existence. Disciplined meditation is the most necessary ingredient for self-discovery and transformation.

Meditation is deep listening. Far from being half-awake grogginess, it is a state of heightened awareness, being alive to your own life, and more importantly, being alive to the possibilities beyond your own life, beyond your material reality. You may think of those possibilities as messages from God, connection to your own inner knowing, or, as Regis puts it, "an expansion of your own consciousness."

Before you learn to expand your consciousness, however, you must learn to be silent and meditation is the discipline that teaches us the value of silence. Meditation allows us to process what is happening and discern what we want to happen. It allows us to clear away the clutter of our daily lives, quiet our minds and perceive on a different level. Although the most common meditation practice involves sitting in a certain position, with your eyes closed, it is not the only way. You may be a person who enters into deep relaxation and intentional receptivity when you run, bike, hike or pray. I have a friend who finds folding clothes an excellent opportunity for meditation. Regis does it while driving.

How you do it is as individual as you are and you may discover that what works for you now is different than what you used to do. The process you use may evolve as you do. There are many ways to reach a meditative state but I believe that daily meditation or a habitual meditative practice is crucial to one's development, crucial for healing and transformation. For in that stillness, in that silence, you are open and receptive to the vastness beyond your conscious physical reality.

I meditate every morning. On days I absolutely cannot begin with meditation, I find some quiet time during the day to center and ground. At home I sit facing east, in front of my altar with lighted candles, my mesa, and other meaningful items. Most of the time I play meditation music in the background, and burn incense. I give thanks for the new day and consciously connect with the divine presence. I light four candles for the four directions, the four elements.

For each element, I say a silent invocation, starting with the South/Fire. "Spirit of the South, Spirit of the Fire, burn away my doubts and fears, my preoccupations and my impatience. Transmute my heavy energy into refined golden light. Ignite in me your passion and compassion, energize me with your sun's rays. Sanctify me. Help me to dare." Then I sit in receptive silence, open to receive from the Fire any message or awareness it may have to offer me. Sometimes the message I receive is related to "daring" or is, perhaps, seemingly unrelated to either the element or the sacred word. Sometimes there is no message at all.

Next is the West: "Spirit of the West, Spirit of the Earth, thank you for abundant life and continued growth. Cleanse and transform me. Receive my heavy energy as fertilizer for your precious soil that brings new life." Then I visualize what I "want" and ask Pachamama to assist me to empower my intention. Often, I visualize a situation as I would like it to happen in the future and, occasionally, a vision comes to me. I open myself up to receive insights. I pause in receptive silence until it feels time to move on.

"Spirit of the North, Spirit of the Air, purify me. Spirit of wisdom, knowledge and grace, blow through me and release all that blocks me from connecting with your infinite vastness. Amplify my awareness and expand my consciousness. Help me to know all that you know." In the North, I feel myself floating in the sky or the cosmos, allowing Air to take me where it will. Some days I simply connect with its pure white divine light. At times, I have insights related to "knowing". I stay in the North until it feels time to move on.

"Spirit of the East, Spirit of the Water, wash me, clean me, sooth me, smooth me, balance me. Help me to be silent." Here I may visualize water, a river or ocean, feeling its soothing energy cleaning and calming me. Other times I will sit in receptive silence. If at any point during the meditation, I feel my mind wondering and making shopping lists, I simply bring my awareness back to the element or the sacred word, as a way of refocusing. I may spend more time with one element than the others on any given day. Some days I feel very connected with many insights and other times less.

Before I come out of the meditation I give thanks for my friends, family and colleagues and I send each of them love and light. I also send healing to people I know who are in need of it, using the symbols we were giving during our initiations. When I open my eyes, I write in my journal including any dreams or insights I had. The whole process generally takes about an hour. This format for my meditation evolved since I began studying the Andean Tradition. When it is possible, I meditate outside using the same basic process. Here in Cusco I meditate in some of the sacred sites in the area. On these occasions I feel the refined energy of the sites and the elements in an even stronger way than when I meditate at home.

This is not at all how I began my practice, however. In 1986 a group from the church I attended was reading a book on Christian disciplines. When I read about meditation, I thought, "I can't do that. I'm too busy in the mornings and at night I'm too tired." Besides, sitting still "doing nothing" didn't appeal to me much. I was busy, busy, busy in those days; I had no time to pause because I didn't want to miss anything. Oddly though (in that none of the other disciplines inspired such a response), I decided grudgingly that I could get up fifteen minutes earlier and I made a pact with myself to meditate for ten minutes every morning for two weeks. That much I could do.

At the end of two weeks, I liked it well enough to continue—having gotten into the habit—though I don't remember having any major insights. It was when I became unemployed nine months later that I started to spend more time meditating each morning as I didn't have to be anywhere else at any certain time. I also started writing my reflections and dreams in a journal after I finished my meditation (which I've done for many years now.) By this point, I was having what I considered daily conversations with God. That was how I heard the message to pay attention during my meeting with Leslie Merlin. It's why I took seriously her impression that I wanted to go to theological seminary. Without that quiet time every day, I might have missed an opportunity that dramatically changed the course of my life.

It was the inner child meditation I did during one healing workshop at the end of 1997 that ultimately lead me to Peru for the first time. Little DiDi told me we needed more adventure and I promised her to do two things a month that were beyond my comfort zone. The first thing I did was attend the lecture in Johannesburg about shamans and healers in Peru. It was then that I knew I had to go to Peru.

I have received many "messages" over the years during my daily meditations, some small and some life changing. The importance of daily practice is that you learn to "hear" more easily the proddings from the spiritual dimension, even though there may be many days when your meditations are quite ordinary or uneventful. Aside from one's daily practice, there are other kinds of meditation that can be used for healing and cleansing, many of which have been mentioned in this book. Some people find "guided meditations" to be quite powerful. This is when someone leads the meditation with general instructions that guide the participants to visualize a safe, loving, peaceful place, to fly, to float, to rest in, to visit your inner child, or connect with God or bring healing light to a specific old wound. There are also the meditations that Regis and Sergio taught us, using the elements of nature: laying face down on the ground and telling "Mother Earth" all your concerns and then turning your ear to the ground to hear her response. You can work similarly while hugging a tree or laying stomach-down on a rock. There are the water meditations, which we have already described. Watching the sun rise and receiving Father Sun's first rays to energize you for the day is a wonderful meditation, as well as a connection to fire that transmutes your heavy energy in its flames.

Whatever way we meditate, when we quiet the chatter of our minds we can hear that other voice within us—the voice of inner knowing, the voice of the ages, the voice of the divine. Through imagination, relaxation, concentration, and visualization problems that seem insurmountable from the mind's point of view can become unraveled. I think of the meditation I had where I saw Glen, the coordinator for our newspaper, Homeless Talk, peacefully handing over the keys and cell phone to me, visualizing the day as I wished it to be. I could never have imagined such a thing with my conscious mind. But my subconscious spoke to my consciousness in that meditation and said, "Such a thing is possible. Live that it be so." And it was so.

Meditation can be both mundane and magical. Sometimes there are meditations where you experience nothing but stillness, other times visions come unbidden, as surprising beautiful gifts from the great beyond. Because you work on the level of image and energy when you meditate, you are able to access time and space non-linearly. You can capture glimpses of the past or the future that have meaning for you in the present.

Shortly before my first trip to Peru I had such a vision during a healing workshop I was leading at the church. I invited all the participants to think of a relationship that needed healing in their lives. We were to meet that person during the meditation and bring divine love and light to them, ourselves, and the situation. I thought of my older brother with whom I had been very close as a child but who had a falling out with me in high school: the relationship was never the same. My intention going into the meditation was to bring healing to our relationship but something else happened once I began meditating.

I saw a vision of my family and myself on the beach in North Carolina. It was a month in the future and we were all there to celebrate my parents' fiftieth wedding anniversary. It was night and we were sitting in a circle around a fire on the beach. I was leading a ritual with them, as a gift to my parents. We started the ritual by each person saying their name, the names of their parents and the names of their grandparents. My three brothers were there with their wives and children. "I am Diane, daughter of Fiora and Norton, granddaughter of Nietta, Dominic, Jack and Mae." The others followed in similar form as we went around the circle. Then each of us said something about ourselves that we were proud of. After that I gave pieces of paper to everyone to write down something that they didn't like about themselves that they wanted to release. When it was their turn they could say what they had written or simply throw it into the fire to be burned. The last round we each shared a fond memory of our time together with the family.

When I came out of the meditation I was stunned by what I had seen. It was such a beautiful ritual and my parents were very moved by it. It felt as if it had already happened even though I wasn't meeting my family in North Carolina until the day after the Conference in Peru ended. We had plans to spend a week together in the same beach house —seventeen of us, eight children (ages 6-17) and nine adults. It would be the first time we were all together for such an extended period of time under one roof. After I had the vision, I felt a strong desire to do that ritual with my family when I saw them. On the other hand, I couldn't really imagine any of them agreeing to do it. It just wasn't their kind of thing. Plus, I wasn't sure we would be able to make a fire on the beach.

Nonetheless, I was comforted by the fact that I knew on some level the ritual had already taken place, whether or not I would actually be able to do it with them. Soon, I was off to Peru and my life was full of other exciting adventures. I flew to New York after the Conference was over, my head still spinning with all the amazing experiences I had there. The next morning, a Saturday I flew to Virginia, and my parents, who had been visiting an aunt, picked me up to drive to the beach together. I told them about many of my experiences and they were surprisingly open and interested.

Then my mother asked me if I would lead a worship service for the family the next day, since there was no Catholic church on the island. I was delighted but also a bit surprised. Everyone in my family is a practicing Catholic and although they had come to respect my ministry and some of them had attended services I had lead, I was still a far cry from being the family priest or spiritual advisor. I said it would be my pleasure but I was inwardly wondering if my siblings and the kids would really go for it.

Each family group arrived on Saturday after long drives, and the energy was a bit chaotic. My first walk down to the beach, I looked to see if there was a spot we might be able to do the fire ritual but there wasn't. I then wondered if the "worship service" might be an opportunity to do some of the things I had envisioned. I set my intention but released any attachment to it. The next morning at breakfast, the children were already in the pool and otherwise dispersed. I casually asked my mother if she still wanted to have a service. She seemed reticent and asked the others what they thought. No one seemed very enthused about the idea but reluctantly agreed to assemble everyone at 11 A.M.. I then found a quiet spot to do my meditation and opened myself to some inspiration. A slightly revised but similar ceremony came to me.

Following the general format of a worship service, the "opening" would be a short prayer then the self-naming. Next the "confession" would be a chance for each person to name something to release. The "offering" would be naming something about ourselves of which we were proud. For each round we would pass the heart stone I found in Peru. I intended to hold the stone that Regis gave me to help me stay centered and open. My idea for "communion", after simple words of institution, would be passing the bread and wine around the circle with each person serving the one on the left. The "closing/blessing" would be the sharing of a fond family memory.

When I finished my meditation, I calmly went downstairs to the living room to set the chairs in a circle and prepare the bread and wine. My mother reminded me it wouldn't be a real mass and perhaps I should forgo communion. I smiled and remained calm. The children were running around and I wasn't sure it was actually going to happen. I remained reasonably calm on the outside, but I was more nervous than when I preached to 850 people in the Johannesburg cathedral. I took lots of deep breaths and remained unattached to the outcome. I knew that it was likely that the group would be resistant to what I had in mind. I called on the Spirit to be present and speak through me. My older brother sat down on my left, which meant that I would be passing the stone to him each time and serving him communion.

Everyone finally settled into the circle, respectfully if not enthusiastically. I prayed aloud for the Spirit to be with us all. Then we began naming ourselves. I wasn't prepared for how touching it was to hear all those names. My parents were named often as a parent or grandparent, which seemed very moving for them. It was wonderful to hear the names of all the other parents and grandparents on both sides of each family. It was as if all of them were present with us for this special occasion. The energy in the circle felt more grounded afterwards. Sharing something they wanted to release was more difficult for some but most of the adults named something, as did some of the children. By the third round,—sharing something we were proud of—I noticed that everyone was fully present and participating. Everyone had such lovely things to say about themselves, especially the children. Even my older brother, who can be quite reserved, seemed to be enjoying the process. I then expounded briefly on Jesus' saying: "When two or three are gathered in my name, I am also there." Passing the bread and wine was very touching and sacred to watch. My six-year-old niece served my father communion, as did others, brother to brother, child to parent or aunt to nephew.

The most beautiful part of all, however, was the last round, sharing a fond family memory. This is when the spirit really took wings and lifted us in her arms. Everyone's heart seemed so open and present and full of joy. I shared about a vacation we took to Florida when I was five and the joy of catching my first fish, learning to swim unassisted, and playing with my older brother in another guest's yellow Karmann Ghia convertible. The delight of everyone grew and grew as each parent and child added memories. I wasn't quite sure what to do when the stone was handed back to me, but then my older brother said, "I have another one!" I happily handed the stone to him and, after he finished, my nephew shouted that he had another one too. Several more people added memories. Then, out of nowhere, I remembered not being invited to a party when I was in my early teens. I was devastated in that way only an adolescent can feel or bear. My older brother came to my room and comforted me, shoring up my faltering self-esteem, gifting me with his love and compassion. I could barely share the memory I was so choked up, recalling the special relationship we had then. I was overcome with love and gratitude for the healing that took place in that moment in the circle. As I tearfully shared the memory, I could feel all the other years of heaviness between us, slip away, leaving only love. I looked over to him and could see water welling up in his eyes also. As a finale, my father, full of tears himself, shared his memory of the day he asked my mother to marry him and to his great delight she said, "yes." I can't remember if we all clapped and cheered but it was the perfect unplanned ending. Interestingly, no one seemed in a great hurry to get up. My parents were beaming. My brother hugged me and thanked me for the wonderful service.

The energy in the house seemed decidedly calmer afterwards. Everyone seemed more relaxed, and happier to be in each other's company. The week went remarkably smoothly. I saw my brother in a new light and our relationship has been much closer since then. The intended healing of that relationship was what began the meditation in Johannesburg, which produced the vision of the fire ritual on the beach. In the fire ritual I had not seen anything specific about my brother and was unable to make any logical connection at the time. Now it was clear. The intention had been manifested.

I could not have created what happened with my own will. Because I had been unattached to whether it happened or how it happened, divine grace was able to work its magic in ways I hadn't foreseen. Did I create the future in my meditation or see into the future to know what would happen? Yes. Does it matter which? No. What matters is the vast unlimited possibilities that exist in the cosmos of which we become aware when we meditate, when we listen, when we are receptive, when we are silent.

Try These Meditations

Basic

Sit comfortably—either cross-legged on the floor or in a chair with your back straight and your feet flat on the floor. Either way your body should be relaxed but your spine straight to align the energy centers of your body. You can play some soothing meditation music if you want or be in silence. Be in a place you are not likely to be disturbed. Light a candle.

Close your eyes and breathe deeply. Inhale and exhale through your nose. Breathe slowly and deeply three times and then return to normal breathing. Relax your forehead, your jaw, your eyes, and your ears. Let the tongue rest behind your lower teeth. Release any tension you have in your neck, your shoulders, and your arms. Let your hands lie comfortably on your legs, palms up and open, relaxed. Release any tension in your stomach, your hips, your knees, and your ankles. Let all your heavy energy flow out through your feet into Mother Earth. Remember that Pachamama receives all your heavy energy as a gift, like fertilizer, that enriches her soil where we plant our intentions so they may grow to fruition.

Be aware of your breathing. Let any thoughts that come in to your mind, flow out again. Observe your thoughts and release them. Stay in the present, focused on your breathing. Relax. Breathe.

Andean

Light four candles for the four directions and the ments. For each direction and element, say a silent in starting with the South/Fire. "Spirit of the South, Spirit of the Fire, burn away my doubts and fears, my preoccupations and my impatience. Transmute my heavy energy into refined golden light. Ignite in me your passion and compassion; energize me with your sun's rays. Sanctify me. Help me to dare." Then sit in receptive silence, open to receive from the Fire any message or awareness it may have to offer you.

Next is the West: "Spirit of the West, Spirit of the Earth, thank you for abundant life and continued growth. Cleanse and transform me. Receive my heavy energy as fertilizer for your precious soil that brings new life." Visualize what you want and ask Pachamama to assist you to empower that intention. Open yourself up to receive insights. Pause in receptive silence until it feels time to move on.

Say to yourself: "Spirit of the North, Spirit of the Air, purify me. Spirit of wisdom, knowledge and grace, blow through me and release all that blocks me from connecting with your infinite vastness. Amplify my awareness and expand my consciousness. Help me to know all that you know." Feel yourself floating in the sky or the cosmos, allowing Air to take you where it will. Stay in the North until it feels time to move on.

Then say to yourself: "Spirit of the East, Spirit of the Water, wash me, clean me, sooth me, smooth me, balance me. Help me to be silent." Visualize water, a river or ocean, and feel its soothing energy cleaning and calming you. Sit in receptive silence.

(If at any point during the meditation, you feel your mind wondering and making lists, simply bring your awareness back to the element or the sacred word, as a way of refocusing. You may spend more time with one element than the others on any given day.)

Inner Child

Start with the Basic meditation. After your body is relaxed and your mind is clear from thoughts, continue to focus on your breathing. Then visualize a bright white light in your heart center. Imagine that light growing bigger and bigger until it surrounds you with white light. Feel yourself floating in the light like a bubble lifting you into space. Float in the bubble of light and know it is the light of the Divine Creator surrounding you with love. Feel that this bubble of loving light is transporting you to a place of beauty and peace, a place where you feel safe and protected and loved. Look around you and see the beauty. Feel the peace. Maybe there are flowers or a river, green grass. Imagine a place that feels like paradise. Make yourself comfortable there. Then invite your inner child to come and be with you. Welcome the child with open arms. (Your inner child is yourself at a young age. Note the age and the attitude of your inner child. Sometimes your inner child will need healing, other times, your inner child will offer you words of wisdom or advice.) Engage in conversation with your inner child: "How are you? How are you feeling?" Listen to the response. Share your own feelings with your child as well. When the conversation seems to be ending (after 15-20 minutes), be sure to thank your inner child for visiting you. Ask if there is something you can do for him/her. Make sure it is something you can do, before making the commitment. Tell your inner child you will be back again to visit. Whenever you are ready imagine once again the white light in your heart center and feel it growing until you are surrounded by the light and lifted up into the bubble. Float in the bubble until you return to where you began. Slowly move your hands and your feet. Be aware of your breathing. Whenever you are ready you can open your eyes.

Wisdom Guide

Start with the Basic meditation. After your body is relaxed and your mind is clear from thoughts, continue to focus on your breathing. With your eyes closed, imagine there is a tunnel of golden light in front of you. Imagine yourself walking into the light, into the tunnel. At the end of the tunnel is a door. Open the door and enter the Temple of Wisdom. It is a beautiful peaceful place. Feel how safe and happy you feel there. It is a place like you have never seen before. There is a very comfortable chair just for you. As soon as you sit down your wisdom guide appears. This wisdom guide can take many forms. Perhaps it is Jesus or your favorite saint or maybe it is another ancient master. The form the guide takes is not what is important. The message is what you have come here for. So ask your question and listen to what the guide has to tell you. When you have asked all your questions and been openly receptive to the response, thank your wisdom guide. Whenever you are ready, move back to the door and re-enter the tunnel of light. Slowly bring your awareness back to the place you are sitting. Slowly begin to move your hands and your feet. Be aware of your breathing. Whenever you are ready you can open your eyes.

Right Brain Writing

This is a slightly different type of meditation. It is designed to move your thinking from the left-brain (practical, linear thinking) to a more creative, free flowing, intuitive kind of thinking. Have with you a pencil, several sheets of paper and something to write on. You will write your question with the hand you normally write with, and then you will put the pencil in your other hand to write the answer. (Your question can be related to something you are struggling with or something that is blocking your desire or it can be just a general question like, "what do I have to learn today?") If you have another question, put the pencil back in your dominant hand and again write the answer with your other hand. The conversation can be between yourself and your inner wise-one. It can be between yourself and God. It can be between yourself and one of your spirit guides. It is up to you.

Begin with the Basic meditation. Once you are relaxed, open and receptive, open your eyes and begin writing.

Sending Light and Love

(This is something you can do at the end of any of these meditations.)

Begin with the Basic meditation. After 15 minutes of open, receptive breathing, visualize the people that you care about. One at a time, send them love and light. Do this with your intention and imagination. Know that the source of this love and light is from the Divine creator. Visualize the light coming into you from the top of your head and feel it coming out of your heart center traveling to the person you care about. When you have finished, think about anyone you know who needs healing and send them love/light as well. Then think of someone with whom you are having difficulties and send them love and light as well. Then send love and light to yourself. Feel it circling in and around you. Soak yourself in this healing image.

Slowly become aware of your breathing. Whenever you are ready you can open your eyes.

Chapter 23: Love

Although "love" is not one of the four sacred words, it is one of the three fundamental principles of life in the Andean tradition: Munay (love), Yachay (wisdom), and Llankay (service). Love is the guiding principle in nearly every religion and spiritual tradition and, ironically, it is simultaneously the most sought after and elusive thing that exists.

Perhaps this is because what most of us call love is predicated on all sorts of terms and conditions. But the truest, purest form of love, divine love, is unconditional love. As with most things, if we've never experienced unconditional love it is hard to conceive of its existence. It's hard for us to imagine that we could be either the givers or receivers of such a thing. Yet it does exist. In fact, it is present all around us, all the time just like the air we breathe. So, why is it so elusive? Maybe, like the song says, we look for love in all the wrong places.

Every Tuesday morning for three years I led a healing workshop, which included a meditation. Although I used many different types of meditation and healing techniques, all of them included making a connection with the unconditional loving presence of the Divine because there is nothing more powerful than unconditional love to heal and transform. I invited people to close their eyes, take a few deep breaths, and release any tension in their bodies. Then I invited them to visualize a glowing white light around their heart center, imagining themselves walking into the light, into a place of peace, where they were safe, protected and deeply loved, a place where God was with them.

In another type of meditation, I invited them to picture someone for whom they cared then, with the power of their intention, send that person love. I could see the smiles on people's faces as they did this. Invariably, tensions released and bodies relaxed. After five minutes or so, I asked them to send love to themselves in the same way. For many people this was much more difficult. Tension would return to their knitted brows; sometimes there would even be tears.

I know it takes practice for people to connect with a divine source that they believe loves them without condition. In most cases this is because they are unable to love themselves without condition. I know it because I have experienced it myself personally as well as professionally. It takes practice because in all meaningful relationships, we need to spend time together in order to know each other, to trust each other. To spend quiet time in the loving presence of the Divine is important because there unconditional love absolutely exists. Once we know unconditional love, really experience it, then we can learn to give that love to ourselves. And once we love ourselves, we can learn to be unconditionally loving with others.

Before I began my work on the Andean path, I was still searching for that perfect love in another person, who I thought would complete me. By the time I had my coca reading with Don Manuel at the turn of the millennium, that yearning no longer existed. When Don Manuel asked me at the end of the reading if there was anything else I wanted to know, it didn't occur to me to ask about a soul mate. It was days after the reading that I realized my omission. That's when it struck me: what I was actually searching for all these years was a different kind of love - love on a higher plane. Through my work with the Andean tradition, I had touched the power of unconditional love and it had transformed me.

I no longer needed that other person because I felt complete within myself. That longing I had for a man to love me was gone. It vanished when I wasn't looking. Something deep and old inside me had been healed and now I loved myself. I loved myself in the way I had envisioned another loving me, with tenderness, acceptance, passion, forgiveness.

When I first met Regis in Urubamba, I asked him what was blocking my desire for connection. His answer to me was all about love: He said, "You are a beautiful person. You have so much love and are very giving. But you can also be gullible. It is good because you are trusting and open, but you have gotten hurt."

He paused and looked at me. "Human beings..." he sighed, "...they do things. Mean, hurtful things sometimes. But that's not what matters. Only love matters, unconditional love. I know men have hurt you in the past but don't hold on to that. That is not what is important. Only love is important. Continue to love unconditionally without expecting anything in return. This is the only thing that really matters." He may not have told me what a strong connection he and I would have in the future, but he did gently nudge me onto the path that eventually allowed me to say 'yes' to that choice.

The longing I had attached to finding my soul mate was really a longing to discover in an ever-expanding way, the vastness of God's creation that I had experienced on the swing when I was three; to tap into that grand force which allows even the impossible to become possible. My desire, my purpose is to learn how to use this power for healing and transformation. In order for us to discover this vastness, we must move out of our woundedness and into another level of consciousness, where we dare to encounter the transformative healing power of divine love that can take us places beyond our imagining.

This is a very different kind of love to what we generally experience in a romantic relationship, or even with friends and family. Romantic or platonic love is usually more conditional, an emotion that we attach to others (or withhold from them) in the hope we will get our needs met. The elusive longing for love that many of us experience is because of these attachments we put on love. When we move to the level of unconditional love the experience is much different. Divine love requires nothing from us. It's ever-present and unending. One very helpful way to experience this kind of love is by working with the elements of nature.

The Andean tradition teaches us to work with the elements of earth, air, water and fire, not only to experience this divine love but also to release all the problems and preoccupations that prevent us from being present to the wonderful possibilities that life is offering us at every turn. Working with the elements helps us to feel restored, centered and aware of who we really are. Human beings are not always capable of reflecting back to us, our truest selves. Nature, and the divine creator, however, are and do. It is their unconditional love, in the midst of our problems and confusion, which enables us to release old patterns that no longer serve us. And from there we can more easily discover what our purpose is in this life. It will also make our relationships with others healthier and more rich.

After moving to Cusco, I had an intense discussion with a young man who had come to speak with me. In the months we had been friends, he told me about his frustration at not being able to find a woman with whom he could spend the rest of his life. We had spoken before about this longing to complete his life with a wife and children to love. This day I was trying to explain that although his desire was a beautiful one, it might actually be preventing him from seeing the gift in other kinds of relationships that he was dismissing because they weren't what he was looking for.

I knew from my own experience that his longing reflected something deep inside himself, not just the desire to find the elusive partner he was sure would give his life purpose and meaning. He called that kind of love, transcendent love. For him it was the ultimate love imaginable. I remembered when I thought so too. I wanted to tell him there was another kind of love even more wonderful; not a fairy tale love but one that could open him up to other ways of knowing, seeing, and being. This love could in fact, lead him (as it had me) to a 'happily-ever-after' kind of existence, with or without his princess.

But I didn't tell him. Like Regis had seen with me, I saw that my friend wouldn't understand me, that it wasn't the right time. I trusted however, that some part of him might be receiving the message on another level and his deeper longing would allow him to discover this in his own time and way.

The conversation made me realize how much I'd changed. Now I was able to see the gift in so many different kinds of relationships, especially with the men in my life, no longer judging them according to some standard of whether they would be suitable mates. People come in and out of our lives for all kinds of reasons, to give us something, tell us something, teach us something. And, since nature's way is always reciprocal, know that we also have something to offer them as well. Even if the relationship doesn't turn out the way we'd like it to, we can recognize the opportunity in it.

Experiencing divine love liberates us. It creates freedom and joy, unattached and unconditional. It opens up new worlds and helps us discover our purpose for being alive, not with our mind or our emotions, but by expanding our consciousness. Look for it in the places it exists, first from the source (God and nature) and then within yourself. After that you will start seeing it everywhere.

Are You Wondering?

How are the elements unconditionally loving?

The elements give you life and breath and warmth and sustenance without judgment or condition. Unlike your parents and teachers, they have no expectations of you. Air, for example is free and available to everyone alike, sinner or saint, day or night. You don't have to earn it. It is everywhere you go, no matter what you do. The same is true of Mother Earth. She is always there, ready to graciously receive your heavy energy, to use it and transform it to enrich the soil of your life. She listens whenever you choose to connect with her and answers if you have ears to hear and time to listen. Trees and plants give you oxygen from your recycled carbon dioxide, free of charge—unconditional. Water washes you, literally and energetically, without terms or expectations. The sun rises everyday – whether you are bad or good- to give you light and warmth. This is the love of the Divine Creator and creation itself. The elements are the vehicles with which the creator loves you into life. Learn to appreciate this unconditional giving, this love, so you can reciprocate in a similar manner. This is what the prophecies called "the time of meeting ourselves again", the coming of the new age where love is the language spoken by all.

Try This

Every morning when you wake up, give thanks to each of the elements for all they give you and to the divine creator for life itself. Smile at the beauty and simplicity of creation's natural order. Feel the freedom in giving and receiving love without condition. Breathe it in and out, love and thanksgiving – for at least 5 minutes before you start your day.

What do you mean "we must move out of our woundedness into another level of consciousness" to experience the vastness of God's creation?

There is so much more to this life than the average person takes time and effort to notice. As you expand your consciousness and amplify your awareness, you begin to see and know more. But if you are stuck inside your ego-self, your hurts and frustrations, your problems and fears, it is as if you are wearing blinders, or viewing life through a small narrow hole in the wall that surrounds you. If you want to broaden your horizons, to experience the vastness, you must simply and clearly let go of all the things that weigh you down and keep your inner vision blocked.

This is why the Andean tradition teaches people to work with the elements. When you release your heavy energy to Pachamama or wash them away in the water, it is like you are hooked up to a dialysis machine. The heaviness is transformed into refined energy that opens up new possibilities and sets you free to explore uncharted waters.

Try This

When you are feeling blocked, frustrated, hurt or angry go outside and lay face down on the ground. Cross your four fingers on top of the four fingers of your other hand and put the tips of your thumbs together, forming a hole for your mouth. Place your forehead down on your hands so your mouth is over the hole.

Make a small space or hole in the ground if the grass is too high. Close your eyes and speak (silently or out loud) to mother earth. Tell her all your problems, concerns and frustrations. When you have told her everything, turn your head and place your ear over the "hole" in your hands and listen to what Pachamama has to tell you. This whole process can take 20-30 minutes.

Chapter 24: Transformation

Practice silence, learn to love, stay balanced in your emotions, and your life will transform. That said, and this being the last chapter, you may think, "Oh, transformation is the goal." I caution you against this notion. Transformation is an on-going process not a final destination.

Instead make love your aim, or peacefulness your intention. Then, whenever you are aware of not being loving or peaceful, become conscious of what is preventing you from being so and gently release it. Be alive in the sacred now. This is the path of transformation.

Transformation happens naturally when you engage in spiritual practice with commitment. It results from your desire to amplify your conscious awareness and reflects your willingness to move beyond what is comfortable for you, to discover how much more there is to life than what meets the eye at first glance.

You may notice changes along the way; things that once made you happy may seem hollow, no longer satisfying. And the small moments and pleasures of life will take on new significance, filling you with joy and reverence that you did not have before. Enjoy these changes; and know they are signs of your evolution.

Some years ago my nephew showed me one of his toys called a transformer. It turned from a slick-looking red sports car into a power-pack robot with arms and legs and a motor for its chest; a kind of Clark Kent-Superman transformation, that moved just as easily one way as the other. The kind of transformation I am talking about doesn't reverse. Once it has occurred there is no going back.

And I promise, you will not want to go back because life becomes richer and fuller if not always easier. I used to worry when I was a theatrical producer: what would be the next project; where would the money come from; would people see my work and be moved by it? When I left producing and became a minister, I still had worries: would the budget be there; would I get approval for projects; would our community members have places to sleep that night? I wanted so much for things to work out as I saw them. My visions felt inspired, so I fought hard for what I thought was right.

All that fighting took so much energy. And I would be terribly disappointed when events didn't pan out as I was sure they were "ordained" to happen. Then I found Regis and Sergio and the Andean tradition, or perhaps they found me. Now events that would have frustrated me even a year ago are simply noted or even causes of wonder. "Oh, that didn't happen the way I thought it would. I wonder what life has in store for me instead." I no longer need to understand every event or analyze every conversation. I live as I am led to live each day more conscious of what emotions are driving my behavior and when I need to release them. I wake up and I spend intimate time tuning in to the divine creator, expanding my consciousness, listening with my heart to inspire my actions. Yes, there are days when my task list is long. Sometimes the actions that need doing, flow like a river. Other times when I'm conscious of pushing too hard with frustrating results, I stop and make time to be still. The old Diane would try to figure out how to do the tasks and then work in a bit of stillness if time permitted. The person I am now knows to follow my inner proddings and to be grateful for the guidance I find in the silence. Many times the situation I was trying to push resolves itself without my doing anything because I have stayed out of the way and allowed the cosmic assistance to work its magic from a viewpoint quite broader than my own. Even if the situation doesn't get resolved, my act of letting go makes me feel more peaceful than frustrated.

This way of being is liberating for me. As I continue to practice and learn, I know there is the possibility that each day can be lived in freedom and peace, even when daily tasks aren't going the way I would like. Perhaps this is what the Inkas meant in the phrase, Taripay Pacha. The "time when we meet ourselves again" is when we create peace and freedom here and now.

I used to ponder what it would mean to become enlightened. When I heard people speak of the next plane of our spiritual development, I envisioned an other-worldly existence where everyone attains incredible knowledge and we all vaporize into happy ether, spirits floating around without need for food or any other creature comforts. That place seemed a long way off to me, virtually unattainable. Now I know that the next level is so close, so within our reach. And I believe it looks pretty much like our world now. There are still groceries and dentists and the need to visit those places because we still inhabit physical bodies. But how we live is very different. We love one another, we value one another, we work together to bring healing to the planet and all of its inhabitants.

Transformation broadens our horizons, opens us up to discover new and greater possibilities. When it occurs, life is no longer what it was, even though the landscape is familiar. Our material reality is the same as it was yesterday and yet everything is different. Transformation is born deep within, changing how we see and feel and relate to things outside ourselves. Because we live in the world differently, often these internal changes cause us to make external changes as well.

It's very exciting to me now to be alive in this moment. The Andean prophecy tells us that this time is the awakening and that the golden age is possible very soon. We can help bring about this new age of peace and harmony by living it now.

I know we can because this is my intention. I know we can because I've seen Regis and Sergio do it, living each day with love and compassion, guided in all things by spirit. I know we can do this because I've seen homeless people in Johannesburg living with dignity, unwilling to let even the most dire of circumstances rob them of humanity. All around the world, at all levels of society, people are learning to live this way, in peace and harmony, even as wars rage and challenges persist.

I asked Regis last summer about the coming of the new age. "The prophecy," he told me, "is clear about dates."

"But what if we say 'no?'" I queried.

"The masters will continue their work of evolving humanity," he said simply. "The people who want it will make it happen. Peace cannot be stopped."

Each one of us present on the planet at this moment has the opportunity to make a difference. I have chosen to work with the Andean tradition because it has assisted me most profoundly in the work of healing and transformation, reverberating deeply in my soul. Regis has chosen this path because he's found it to be the most natural, the most complete for him. The Andean spiritual tradition is not a religion. It is a practice that helps us to connect with divine love and light, a principle central to most major religions. Therefore, the practices I have described here can be done by people no matter what their religion. Many Andean "priests" in Peru arc also practicing Catholics. The most important thing is that your spiritual path or religion or faith tradition helps you attain love and peacefulness. How you do it does not matter. That you do it matters a great deal. Whichever path you choose, enter it with reverence and with commitment. Work to become conscious and mindful of each moment.

This is what I believe Jesus meant when he said the Kingdom is at hand. At hand, our hands, in our hands, and within our grasp. You can choose to live in the "kingdom" whether the person next to you makes the choice or not. You do not need to change that person's mind. That is not your job. Your most important work concerns yourself. It is a sign of your own transformation when you stop trying to transform any other. When you change, the world around you will shift. You can feel it and see it. Those who know you will be able to feel it and see it in you. Some of them will change because of it, some will not. But as more and more of us choose to live this way, human consciousness will change. Universal transformation will occur when love and peace reach critical mass. At a certain point, there will be no other way to live and still be part of society.

To embrace change is to begin the process of transformation. Everyday things change; the seasons move in their cycles, the corn is planted, grown and harvested; our body's cells die and replace themselves. And yet, inertia drives us to keep as much as possible the same. Even when life is no longer working well for us, we often hang on hoping it will get better tomorrow. So we change our clothes, our car and the décor in our room instead of changing the patterns that keep us trapped in the status quo. To dare, to move beyond our comfort zones, is to rock inertia, to embark on a road, not simply to change the routines of our life but to permanently alter how we engage with them.

Why give up comfort for transformation? Because, no matter where you are right now, life is so much more than you can imagine, so much fuller, richer, and more magical. If you want to discover the depths of life, the depths of your inner being, you can set in motion the process of transformation with the power of your intention. As you do this, the knowledge you need is presented to you, offered at every turn. Each time you say yes, the next door or window opens. If my transformation process is any indication, the adventure is not always smooth and easy, nor the outcomes always as you might hope. But to engage in the process is always rewarding, always more and better than what you are leaving behind. Always.

To transform is to become totally new while remaining yourself. In fact, transformation enables you to become your truest self, that for which your soul searches and longs to become. The more you discover about your best self, the more inspired you become to continue on the path of transformation. The radiance within you begins to shine so brightly that it lights the path for others to also find their way.

Engaging in this process raises your consciousness, heightens your level of awareness. Like the difference between your television's antenna and cable hook-up to a satellite dish, you become able to tune in to other frequencies that allow you to see more, feel more, experience more.

But of course, it is up to you. Is that what you want? Are you delighted by the thought of pushing through inertia? Are you happy to release your heavy load to the loving arms of Mother Earth? Are you ready to give up what feels familiar in order to soar on the winds of wisdom, to sail on the waters of tranquility, to ignite your passion for discovering new possibilities? Do you want to help create the golden age of peace and prosperity? Is that what you want?

Say yes, and all of this becomes possible. All of this and more.

Epilogue

Wendy and I began writing this book in 2000 and modified it in 2002. We spoke with many agents and publishers during that time who liked the book but didn't think it had a sufficient market so we ended up self-publishing and selling it on line and at the Inka workshops we continue to do with Regis and Sergio in South Africa, Canada, USA and Peru.

I had thought when I moved to Cusco in 2000 that the book would be a vehicle for us to promote the vision of the Centro Espiritual. I envisioned a popular best seller. I also thought that a wealthy donor I knew would give us the money to buy land in the Sacred Valley for the Center. Neither of those things happened. (Yet.)

One day (before I had heard from the donor), I decided to go to the Sacred Valley to the Inka ruins in Pisac. I had been there several times (first during the Millennium Journey) and liked the energy of that mountain. I brought watercolors with me to paint.

The night before I had an interesting dream. I was on a stone path walking up. There was a Puckish young Inka guide dressed in a tunic who was silently urging me to follow him. Up and up he went with me ten paces behind him, climbing. The path was rugged but had stone steps. Finally he stopped and gave me the number 44. Then he said, "Now you have the keys to the portal." I woke up with a start, knowing that something important had happened. This feeling stayed with me as I traveled on the bus 15 miles to Pisac.

I took a taxi up the back way to the ruins. The temple area sits atop an 11,000 ft. mountain surrounded on all sides by Inka terraces, 1,000 ft. above the town. Instead of going to the temple site, I decided to wander around the mountain to find a quiet spot to sit and paint and eat my picnic lunch. After several hours of basking in the sunshine and the refined energy of the mountain, I decided to walk down the front of the mountain to the town below. I was following my instinct because I didn't know the way.

As I walked, I began finding heart stones. Lots of them. So many in fact, that I thought it was a sign to pay attention. Then I found a perfectly flat stone about 2 inches square in the exact perfect form of a heart. It was a pinkish stone with flecks of something that sparkled like gold. I stopped in my tracks. Then I realized with a pounding heart that the path I was walking down was the exact one I had been climbing in my dream! In the dream I had no view except the upward incline of the stone path, but now I was walking down and directly in front of me was the farm that Regis and I had wanted to buy for the Center. Just to the left of it was another farm, but much smaller. Both had the river on one side and the sacred mountain on the other, just like the land in Regis' vision. I was sure in that moment that we would get the money to buy the big farm and build the center there. Perhaps we still will because that land remains for sale after 6 years.

But as often happens when you are open to divine grace, the story took an interesting turn.

I was disappointed when we didn't get the money but not discouraged. I thought, "The Centro Epsiritual was a vision, something that Regis had seen. It exists some time in the future. Let go of the "business plan" and trust that it will unfold when the time is right."

Instead of raising money to buy land, I focused my attention on networking with people and organizations from various religions and spiritual traditions from around the world that were also interested in reorienting the collective consciousness of humanity toward love, light, truth, peace and unity.

For two and a half years I lived in Cusco doing this work. I continued to practice and learn alternative healing. I organized workshops and initiations for Regis and Sergio in Peru and North America. Life was interesting and full. But I was ready to have my own place. I went to see the owner of the land in Pisac to see if he would sell me a small piece but he didn't want to sub-divide. I looked for other land in the Valley but my heart was really in Pisac.

Then by chance, I met Ruben, the farmer next door, who wanted to sell his land. It was the other farm I could see that day I found my heart stone. He agreed to sell me a small part of it and I built my house of mud and wood, stone and glass. As these things go, it went over budget and by the time I moved in at the end of 2002, I was nearly out of money. So I decided to rent to tourists my small cottage and my two guest rooms to make some money. I put up a few signs and started getting people, lovely people interested in spiritual things.

I had bought enough land from Ruben to build a conference center but that would have to wait until I had more money. In March of 2003, during my morning meditation, I got a message. "Build the extra rooms first." The architectural plans included a building with 4 extra guest rooms to the side of the main conference area. This would certainly be cheaper to do. I spoke to my parents about loaning me the money.

Two days later I was with a friend at a café in Pisac when a woman began talking with us and asked if there were any new hotels in Pisac. It turned out that she was updating the Lonely Planet guide for Peru. I took her to see my house, which she loved and promised to include it in the guidebook. I told her I was planning to build some more rooms. I had to make up a name on the spot. That's how Paz y Luz (Peace and Light) B&B was born. By the time the Lonely Planet was released, the new rooms were ready. She wrote that Paz y Luz was a spiritual place run by a woman who does mystical tours. I couldn't have asked for better advertisement. What a delight it is to have a "business" where interesting people from around the world happen upon my doorstep.

Soon Ruben sold the rest of his farm to other people who began building houses. As fate would have it, one of my new neighbors is Joyce. We had a strong connection when we met and after she read my book in English, she felt compelled to translate it into Spanish. We were planning to print it to sell ourselves, like the English version. But one day last year her daughter was visiting here with some friends from Lima who worked for Planeta Publishing Group. After reading it, they agreed to publish the book but thought it needed more material. It was Joyce's idea to put questions and answers at the end of each chapter and to give people practical exercises to do. Aside from making the book more engaging, it gave me a chance to review my own process and to make sure I am practicing what I preach. Thank you Joyce. We shall see how the story unfolds.

Last year, thanks to a generous gift from my parents, Paz y Luz has expanded and now has its conference room. It is circular and glass-walled with a spectacular view of the Pisac ruins. If you look carefully, you can faintly see the stone path of my dream where I found the sparkling heart stone. You can also see the spot where I sat by the fire the Millennium midnight with the intention of manifesting a book and a spirituality center.

As my friend Wendy says, "God gives you everything you ask for and nothing you expect."

Don't think you are reading this book by accident. However it came to you, it is in your hands for a reason. Experiment, search, cleanse and release. Move beyond your comfort zone to discover your inner wisdom. Remember that the universe, with all its elemental powers is conspiring to assist you every minute of every day. Believe it, and you will feel it, see it, and learn to fly on its wings. I promise you that the excitement of your adventure will be matched by your desire and willingness to follow its urging.

Step through the gateway now.

ACKNOWLEDGEMENTS

There are three people I would like to thank for making this book a reality.

Firstly, my dear friend Wendy Crumpler, a gifted writer, teacher and artist – Writing this book with her taught me the joy and freedom of true collaboration and the power of unconditional love and acceptance. Thank you Wendy.

Secondly, Joyce Canny de Palma, who trusted her intuitive call to translate the book into Spanish as a form of *anyi* for her Peruvian friends, so they could learn from their own indigenous tradition. It was through Joyce that the book reached the hands of Planeta Publishing Group. Thank you Joyce.

Finally, I want to thank Sergio Vilela, editor of *Grupo Planeta* in Lima for all his hard work to publish this book. Thank you Sergio for believing my story has a market in both Spanish and English, here in Peru and elsewhere.

****

I also want to express my deep appreciation to Kamaq Weageq (Regis) and Hatun Runa (Sergio), powerful masters of the Andean Tradition, for the teachings that transformed my life. Thank you Regis and Sergio for your patience and generous giving of your time and love and wisdom, that so many may benefit from these ancient practices.

If you have questions or comments or would like to know more about future Inka Spirituality workshops, please write me at dianedunn@terra.com.pe or cuscodiane@hotmail.com